Badass Babes of the Bible

Drenda Thomas Richards

Badass Babes of the Bible

Copyright © 2021 **Drenda Thomas Richards**

ISBN 978-1-7368217-0-1

First paperback edition March 2021

First ebook edition March 2021

Book cover and interior design by JohnEdgar.Design

Dedication page photo courtesy: Ann-Marie Smalley

This Work Is For

The women and men in the adult entertainment industry.

Thank you for allowing me into your clubs and into your lives.

My life is forever changed.

Thank you.

Contents

WOMEN OF ACTION

Rahab...3

Jehosheba.. 8

Abigail... 12

Jael 16

WOMEN OF FAITH

The Bleeding Woman 23

Esther..27

Hannah..30

Ruth 32

The Widow of Zarephath................................35

Lydia 40

Elizabeth...42

DISRUPTORS

Shiphrah & Puah...47

Moses' Queen Mum, Hatshepsut....................49

Aksah...52

Woman at the Well 54

Mary - Mother of Jesus 57

Mary of Bethany 60

WOMEN WITH A MESSAGE

Judge Deborah 65

Priscilla 68

Dorcas..71

Prophetess Anna...74

Phoebe..76

WOMEN WHO STOOD STRONG IN ADVERSITY

Tamar..81

Jochebed 84

Leah...86

Rachel...89

Hagar 92

Mary Magdalene 96

WOMEN WHO REPENTED

She Got Caught...101

Martha..104

Miriam...107

MISGUIDED BABES

Eve 113

Bathsheba 115

Gomer 118

(The Other) Tamar....................................120

Sapphira..124

Sitidos, Wife of Job...................................127

Jezebel..130

Rebekah 134

Delilah 138

WARNING

EXPLICIT LANGUAGE

This book contains language some
might find unsuitable.
If that's you, put this book down now.
Read no further.
This book isn't for you.

&

Don't bother writing the author
about your concerns.
She didn't write this for you.

Foreword

From a time when women

were considered to be property,

had no voice,

were glorified slaves,

whose worth was based on the number of children they produced

come stories of Badass Babes who did ordinary things with extraordinary outcomes.

These Badasses didn't care what their culture said, nor did they concern themselves with who others declared them to be.

They stepped out.

They pursued their dreams.

Some almost gave up on their dreams, but then it happened!

Like in real life, bad stuff happens too. Inside these pages, you'll find stories of bravery and victory, but you'll also find stories of rape, incest, and murder.

Some Badasses were only mentioned once and never heard from again—at least not in the scriptures. I believe they continued to influence their environment in badass ways.

All of these incredible women provide lessons for us today. We can learn from the good, the bad, and the ugly because we all have good, bad, and ugly within us.

Many of the Badasses you'll read about just wanted to be loved and accepted. Isn't that just like you and me today? Please know you're enough just as you are. You are worthy of every good thing your heart desires. You don't have to earn anyone's love. Be you, Badass Boo.

I trust you'll see your Badass self within these pages and have the courage to dream big or learn to dream again. I want you to know there's a God who loves you, who is rooting for you, who has a plan and purpose for your life, and who is working everything out for your good. It's never too late to pursue your purpose, your dharma.

Everything is 100% possible, 100% of the time.

Now, get on with your Badass self!

Women of Action

These Badass Babes didn't sit around waiting for things to happen; they took matters into their own hands! Their badass bravery changed the lives of the people around them and for generations after.

Rahab

(Joshua 2 & 6)

BUT FIRST, SOME BACKGROUND:

Moses died, and Joshua became the new leader of the Jewish people. It was time to enter the Promised Land, but to get there, they had to take over some cities. The first was the city of Jericho. It had high and thick walls. No one went in, and no one came out. It looked hella intimidating. God promised Joshua the city would be his and gave him a unique strategy, but, being a good military commander and probably a little skeptical, Joshua first sent two spies to scope out what was going on inside those walls.

I'm basically one of *People* magazine's most beautiful women, and I own a successful business. I'm an innkeeper and a madam—my inn also functions as a brothel. It's one of the most popular places in town. Clean rooms, good food, fine wine, and even finer women. I have quite the reputation, and the one place in town with only five-star reviews.

3

As you can imagine, lots of secret business deals and war plans happen here because these walls don't talk. Military soldiers are some of my best customers. They like to unwind here, and when men get comfortable, they get chatty.

Two new men came into my place the other night. It's obvious they are spies, and they work for Joshua and those wandering Israelites. I've heard about them. Who hasn't? The Red Sea parted for them. They have water in the desert. They are God's Chosen People. I'm definitely not going to do anything to offend them.

Word gets out to my king, and he sends soldiers to capture the spies. I take the spies to my roof and hide them under the barley from a recent harvest. I hope they aren't allergic or have hay fever. It could kill them. Or they could sneeze, and it could kill me. Just as I get them comfortable and hidden, there's a knock at the door downstairs. *Cue the dramatic music: dun dun duuunnnn*

I answer the door, and it's the king's soldiers. They push their way in asking where the spies are. I keep my cool. After all, I'm a badass businesswoman. I can handle a few soldiers.

"Yeah, some guys showed up here, but I didn't know where they were from. You fellas know as well as anyone, we get a lot of people coming through. They left at dusk right before the city gate was shut. You must have just missed them. If you go after them now, you might catch them." The soldiers take off in pursuit of the spies.

I go back upstairs and tell the spies I have a great respect for them and their people. Everyone in town is afraid of them and on edge because we can see them camped on the other side of the river. We're just waiting for them to pounce.

The savvy businesswoman in me sees an opportunity I can't pass up, and I make a deal with them: I saved their lives tonight. In return, they have to save me and my family when they take over the city. They agree.

I let them out by lowering a rope through a window. No one sees them because the inn is part of the city wall. I tell them to hide in the hills for three days because that's how long it will take those soldiers to get back here. After three days, they can go whatever way they want to get home.

Before they leave, we make final plans on how they're going to save me. I'm supposed to tie a red rope in the same window I just let them down from. If that rope isn't there, or if all of my family are not with me when things go down, they don't have to save us. Deal. As soon as they leave, I tie that red rope in the window. I'm taking no chances.

Several days later, all, and I mean *ALL*, of the Israelites start marching around the city. It's very strange. They say nothing the entire time—just march around the entire city wall once, and then leave. Freaky. They've got to be up to something, but what?

They come the next day and do the same thing—once around the city wall, then nothing. These people are crazier than I thought. After six days of this, we're used to it. We're saying to each other, "Oh, it's just the crazy neighbors again. They'll be gone soon. Ignore them."

Then comes day seven. The Israelites start their usual march around the city. Once around and they'll be gone… but they're still here. They circle a second time. A third time. This can't be good. Something's up. A fourth time. My family better get their butts to my place, and quick. Shit's about to go down.

The seventh time around, the priests start blasting their trumpets, and the people who have been marching around the city start yelling and shouting.

It's going down all right. Literally. The walls of our city come crashing down. They came in like a wrecking ball. People are being smashed and buried underneath the ruble. Donkeys, sheep, and cattle are dying, too. It's horrible.

My family and I are huddled together waiting. Listening. Watching. I see the spies coming towards us, so I scramble and wave the red cord. They come rescue me and my family just like they promised. Then they burn the whole city behind us. These guys don't take prisoners. They just kill 'em all.

I live with the Israelites for the rest of my days. Why wouldn't I? They saved my life that day. I don't just live with them, though. I become one of them and part of their culture. I have a son named Boaz—he's a real stand-up guy.

I'm one of five women mentioned in Jesus' heritage—he's a direct descendant of mine. People refer to me as "the prostitute," but I prefer to think of myself as a Badass. I stared death in the face and didn't blink.

LIFE APPLICATION:

- God doesn't care what your occupation is. He cares about you.
- God keeps his promises, even when it feels like all of the walls are crumbling around you.
- Be impeccable with your word.
- Kick fear in the face.

Jehosheba

(2 King 11:2 and 2 Chronicles 22:10-12)

My stepmother is a wicked witch. No, really, she is. She comes by it honest because her parents were two of the wickedest rules ever—Ahab and Jezebel. People even refer to some women today as "Jezebels." Still famous after all of these years. And this fruit didn't fall far from its tree. Talk about bad blood...

Queen A (her name is Athaliah, but that's a mouthful) is on a rampage. Her son, my stepbrother, was killed, and she's out for blood. But she's not out to kill the people who killed her son. Oh no, that's not wicked enough—she's killing her own sons and grandsons! I told you, she's Wicked with a capital W. Why would she kill her own blood, you ask? Because she doesn't want any descendants of David on the throne. Word is, the Messiah (Jesus) will come from David's bloodline, which we're part of, and she doesn't want that. She worships a different god and totally has it out for us Jews.

Her soldiers are roaming through the palace and streets

looking for male members of the royal family. They've rounded up several princes, including my infant nephew, in order to kill them. I can't let that happen. I bide my time and try to look casual, and when no one is looking, I grab the infant carrier with Joash inside. His nurse is standing nearby, and I motion for her to follow me. We count on the chaos and all of the extra people in the palace to distract everyone as we slip away.

Now, where do we go? I only think for a moment. I know the perfect place—my house. Queen A will NEVER go there! My husband is the high priest. We live in a temple. People refer to us as "The Princess and the Priest." Pretty catchy, right? And convenient—Queen A won't step foot into God's house. *Can't touch this!*

We tell no one about Joash. The Queen seems to have forgotten he exists. He secretly lives with us for six YEARS. How we pull this off, I'll never know. Well, I do know—divine intervention. God helped us. Joash is such a good boy. He never complains or wonders why he can't go outside and play. We make his life as normal as we can, but honestly, each day is a challenge. When he turns seven, we make a decision. My husband swears commanders, mercenaries, and palace guards to secrecy and makes an elaborate plan that will impact the future of our nation. It will also get us killed if one little thing goes wrong or if anyone talks.

Today is the day. The palace guards (armed to the hilt with weapons) surround the throne, the temple, and the altar. They have orders to kill anyone who tries to break through. It's time for The Big Reveal. My husband walks out with Joash. The palace guards surround him as

9

he walks to the altar. When he stops, my husband places the crown on his head and presents him with a copy of God's laws. He anoints him and proclaims him to be king. Everyone starts clapping and shouting, "Long live the king!" Trumpets are blaring. People are dancing. It's like Mardi Gras on steroids. Go big or go home, right?

Queen A hears the noise and runs to the temple to find out what's going on. When she sees the newly crowned king, she freaks out. She tears her clothes and starts shouting, "Treason! Treason!" But we're prepared for her. My husband orders the commanders to take her to the soldiers in front of the temple and to kill anyone who tries to interfere. The soldiers seize her and take her out to the gate, and that's where they kill her.

Joash rules for forty years. It makes my heart happy every time I see him on that throne. I know how things could have been. People tell me how brave I was to do that, but I don't see it that way. I know God promised that the Messiah would come through David. I knew if I didn't act in that moment, it would all be over. I didn't want that on my conscience. It was in my power to do something, so I did.

LIFE APPLICATION:

- When it's within your power to do good, you must act.
- Fear and courage can reside inside you at the same time.
- Kick fear in the face!
- Do it scared.

- Do the right thing no matter the consequences.

Abigail

(1 Samuel 25)

BUT FIRST, SOME BACKGROUND:

What do you do when you've married a fool? Like, literally—her husband's name actually meant "fool," and it was painfully accurate. Abigail, on the other hand, was beautiful and wise. Somehow the poor girl ended up married to Nabal the Fool. At least he was rich, I guess. It was a toxic relationship, but she couldn't leave because she was considered to be his property, not her own person. Such bullshit, right?

David (the future king) is on the run from the murderous current king, Saul. Everyone in the country knows it. While on the run, David protected my husband's shepherds and their flocks from thieves and murderers—literally formed a human wall to protect them. Nice guy, right? Now David and his men are nearby and hungry, so David sends some of his servants to ask Nabal for food and drink. It does not go well.

Nabal, fool he is, mocks David's servants. He even says,

"Who's David?" and "How do I know y'all are for real? Why should I give you anything?"

David's servants go back and tell David what Nabal said, and David, clearly hangry and not to be trifled with, says, "Get your swords. Nabal is a dead man, and so is everyone around him."

Meanwhile, one of the servants comes to tell me what Nabal has said and that he also heard David was on his way to wipe all of us out. I'm not one to sit around and just let things happen. I'm a woman of action. I tell the servants to prepare a bunch of food and wine to send to David and his men. Even though Nabal is a crazy fool of a man, he's my husband, and I want to protect him, our servants, and our livelihood. Real talk, though, it's totally self-preservation. I know David is out for revenge, and he will wipe out everything in sight. Including me. And I don't particularly want to die today.

Once the gift of food and wine is on its way to David, I jump on my donkey and ride towards David and his army—and possibly my death. Feel free to refer to me as a brave and badass babe, now.

I see David approaching, and I get off my donkey and bow low before him. I want to make a good first impression so that he listens to what I have to say. I tell him that I know my husband is a fool, and I offer the gift of food as an apology for Nabal's behavior. He seems receptive, so I continue. "You don't need to have Nabal's death on your conscious. He was merely being himself—a fool—so you definitely have an opportunity to be the bigger person here." I ask for forgiveness for my husband's actions, and I also reminded David that he's the future king. Clearly far above this fool husband of mine.

Thankfully I'm pretty persuasive (I'd totally rock on a debate team), and David realizes the truth in my words. He thanks me for my good judgement and drops his vendetta against Nabal. Hallelujah!

Satisfied that I have skillfully avoided the disaster my fool husband had almost created, I head back home. Where I find an extremely drunk Nabal throwing a party. Because he's a dumbass. The next morning, when he's sobered up, I tell him how close he'd come to death and how I had saved his sorry ass. When Nabal realizes how close he actually came to losing everything, he has a heart attack, falls into a coma, and dies 10 days later. Smartest thing he ever did.

David hears Nabal has died and decides to shoot his shot—he sends word that he wants me for his wife. Hell yeah! I'm no fool—I know a good offer when I get one. Someone bring the donkey around, I'm out! But I won't forget the people who helped me while I was married to Nabal, so I have five of my servants pack up and go with me to join David. We're moving on up!

Real Housewife of Israel: I might have been married to Nabal the Fool, but I'm Nobody's Fool. I know how to take care of myself and my friends. Stick with me, and you'll end up in the palace.

LIFE APPLICATION:

- **Be kind and gracious to everyone.**
- **Keep your peace (and, thus, your head).**

- You reap what you sow, so make sure it's quality.
- If you take responsibility for today, you take control of your destiny.

Jael

Judges 4:17-26

BUT FIRST, SOME BACKGROUND:

For twenty years, King Jabin of Canaan had cruelly oppressed the Israelites. The Prophetess Deborah (a Badass Babe in her own right) told Barak, the military commander, that he should gather troops and go into battle against Sisera, commander of Jabin's army. Barak and the Israelites would be victorious, but ultimately the defeat of Sisera would come at the hands of woman. And so it did.

There's a battle raging not far from here between the Canaanites and the Israelites. It doesn't really have anything to do with us Kenites, to be honest. My husband, Heber, is friendly-ish with King Jabin, but I have zero respect for that man. You wouldn't believe the cruelty he encourages his people to inflict on the Israelites. It turns my stomach. There's not much I can do about it, but man, oh man... if I had the chance to do something to change it, I'd take it in a heartbeat. It makes me so angry and makes

16

me feel so helpless. The Israelites are good people, and they've already been through so damn much.

We get word that the battle has turned in favor of the Israelites—and I do a little happy dance—but we don't expect any of the fighting to come near us. Heber assures us that our little tent village is perfectly safe, and I believe him. There are some rumblings that Sisera may have escaped the battlefield, but I ignore that. Probably just hopeful musings of some Canaanite sympathizer.

I'm walking back to my tent when I hear a rustling. A man is moving between tents, trying to stay hidden. I watch him curiously for a few moments before I realize who he is—Sisera. That cockroach of a man is mere steps away from me. He looks at me and our eyes lock. I have a split-second to make my decision.

I smile at him—demurely but a little saucily too. And try not to vomit in my mouth. If he believes me to be friendly, he'll let his guard down. "Come, my lord," I say to him. "Come right in. Don't be afraid." I gesture into my tent. I should get an f'ing Oscar for this performance. He looks, well, like a man who just escaped a raging battle. And smells like it, too. UGH. I gesture for him to lie down, and I cover him with a blanket.

"I'm thirsty," he says in a gravelly voice. Too bad I don't have any poisoned wine handy. I smile. I open a skin of milk and let him drink from it. He tells me to stand in the doorway of my tent while he rests, and if anyone asks, there's no one in my tent. I tell ya, military commanders think they're the boss of everyone.

As I wait for him to fall asleep, I gather my courage.

What I'm thinking about doing—what I'm about to do—I don't want to think about what will happen if I don't pull this off perfectly. I have to be sure. I slip back into my tent, my heart hammering so loudly in my chest that I'm sure the sound of it will wake him. I look down at him for a moment, and I'm filled with such an overwhelming need to avenge the Israelites. Then I act swiftly. I push the sleeping Sisera right off in the floor. That'll let me know for sure he's good and asleep. When he doesn't wake, I take a tent stake in one hand and a hammer in the other. I take a deep breath and drive the stake right into the bastard's temple. Straight through and into the ground. Turns out I'm stronger than I thought—literally and figuratively.

The air in my tent is heavy with the coppery smell of blood, and I step outside to draw in a deep breath of fresh air. I see Barak coming toward me, looking for Sisera, no doubt. When he gets close enough, I softly call to him. "Come," I tell him, "I'll show you the man you're looking for." He looks doubtful, but he follows me into my tent where I show him Sisera's body. Barak looks at Sisera and then at me. I'm sure he doesn't know quite what to think. Then he takes a couple of steps backwards. "You're safe. I'm fresh out of stakes," I laugh. "Milk anyone?"

Narrator in the voice of Lady Whistledown:

Dear Reader, You could said Jael NAILED IT. Word has it—in more ways than one.

LIFE APPLICATION:

- Use what's in your hand/available.
- Act! Don't hesitate.
- You're stronger than you think.

Badass Babes of the Bible

Women of Faith

Faith is a quiet strength.
These Badass Babes showed extraordinary faith despite going
through some hard stuff, and that faith was rewarded.

The Bleeding Woman

(Luke 8:43-48)

BUT FIRST, SOME BACKGROUND:

In biblical times, when a woman had her period, she was labeled "unclean." Anything she touched was unclean, and anyone who touched her was unclean. Everything she sat on or laid down on was unclean. It was her responsibility not to contaminate others. In fact, her "impurity" lasted seven days beyond the last day of bleeding.

Now imagine what it must be like to bleed for TWELVE YEARS STRAIGHT. EVERY. DAMN. DAY. Talk about PMS! No girls' night out. No day at the spa. No manis or pedis. Just living in isolation on the outskirts of town.

Outcast.

Abandoned.

Alone.

Bleeding.

    No one knows why I'm bleeding. Doctors rip me off trying to "fix" me. And the other things they do to me saying they're "helping" me? Despicable.

Disease, desperation, disappointment, disillusionment...

Until one day I hear about a man. A Healer. I have nothing to lose.

I see and hear the crowd as it passes by my tent. How can I not? This guy and his posse of 12 have attracted a lot of attention, and the crowd rivals Bourbon Street at Mardi Gras. I follow along, staying towards the back of the crowd so that no one will see me and force me to go back home. My heart races, and I desperately just need to get near this healer. I KNOW there's something different about this man.

Finally, I get my chance. I push my way through the crowd and grab for his garment. My fingertips catch his hem as people are pushing and shoving all around me.

My bleeding stops.

The man stops.

He turns.

"Who touched me?" he asks.

His posse looks at him like he's crazy. "What'd'ya mean who touched you? There are hundreds of people here pushing and shoving."

I shrink back.

He sees me. He. Sees. ME... shit.

I'm sure I'm about to have a heart attack, and I kind of wish the ground would just open up and swallow me. But I've come this far. I take a deep breath and walk toward him.

His eyes bore into me. My voice cracks as I tell him I was desperate and had to touch him. I'm afraid of his reaction. This is what a heart attack feels like, right? Just my luck that I'm gonna drop dead thirty seconds after I finally stop bleeding. What a cosmic joke.

Silence sweeps through the crowd as everyone waits to hear his response. If he's pissed, I'm probably about to be stoned to death. Great. Definitely should have just stayed in my tent. I mentally shrug my shoulders and think, '*At least they'd be putting out of my misery.*' What can I say? After 12 years, I've developed a dark sense of humor.

"Daughter."

Wait. WAIT. What? He called me daughter? He called me *daughter*. No one has claimed me in twelve years. But this stranger is calling me daughter. Now my heart is about to explode with joy. What a rollercoaster.

I give myself a mental shake. *Pay attention, dummy. He's still talking...* He says my faith has healed me, has saved me, and I can go in peace.

Peace.

No more bleeding. That's peace.

No more being called unclean. That's peace.

No more isolation. That's peace.

Faith. Touch. Healed. Daughter. Peace.

LIFE APPLICATION:

- **You belong when you say you belong. You don't need anyone's permission.**

- One touch, one word, one encounter can change everything if you have faith.
- Persevere, be bold, and move your feet. You're a badass babe. Don't be afraid to take care of yourself.
- Desperation isn't always bad. It can create motivation and opportunity in places you might not expect.

(Her own Badass Book in the Bible)

BUT FIRST, SOME BACKGROUND:

King Xerxes of Persia was having a party with his friends and they were all drunk. Had been for seven days. He ordered Queen Vashti to appear before him and his buddies in the nude to show off her beauty. She refused and, because she dared to disrespect him and his guests like that, she was banished from the throne. Now the King is seeking a new queen.

The kingdom is abuzz with the news of Queen V getting the boot. Now all of the fair young virgins are in competition to be the next queen. We are put up in a fancy house at the palace grounds. Each day is filled with high-end spa treatments for face, hair, body, and nails. A personal chef makes the finest of foods. Make-up artists and hair stylists are assigned to each girl. It's fabulous. I never want this to end.

We live like this for a year, and it's like nothing I've ever known. I've caught the king's eye, and he starts sending me gifts, and I'm moved to the nicest room in the house. I'm trying not to get ahead of myself, but this is a promising development. I could actually be the next queen!

Me, queen. It's almost absurd. I was raised by my cousin Mordecai, my father's nephew. Every day he walks by the gate to the house to check on me, giving me tips on what to say and do. He helps keep me grounded, too. I don't need to let all of this go to my head—I need to remember my faith and where I came from. He tells me not to say anything about my family or the fact that I'm Jewish, though. They don't need to know. Either you pick me, or you don't. I would miss the special treatment though...

It's time for the king to make his decision—basically the final rose ceremony. The King is smitten by me and places a crown on my head. He still doesn't know who I really am.

Life is good until Haman, the number two man in the Kingdom, puts a hit out on the Jews—my people—because he hates Mordecai. And all because Mordecai refused to bow to him. Petty.

I ask Mordecai what I should do because I can't approach the King without an invite. Even as queen, it's literally illegal and punishable by death. What a dumb rule, but alas, it is what it is.

Mordecai tells me I can't remain silent. I have to protect my people, and maybe I was made queen for such a time as this. Whoa. Pump the brakes. That's a lot to process. I tell him to give me three days. Tell everyone to fast for three days. I will, too. Then I'll go to the king. If I die, I die.

Three days later....

I put on my royal robes. I try to be confident. My insides are jelly, but I'm looking like a million bucks. Fake it 'til you make it, right? I hang out in front of the throne room so Xerxes can't miss me. He sees me and invites me in. He's still smitten, and he tells me I can have anything—even half of his kingdom. Maybe this will work out after all.

I take a deep breath and tell my story. I tell him that I'm Jewish; I tell him about Mordecai; I tell him that his henchman, Haman, is planning to kill me and my people. I know he's going to be angry, but I'm not sure if it will because I'm Jewish or because Haman is a murderous jackass.

Long story short, my people are saved. Haman is hanged in the very gallows he had built for Mordecai. The King gives me Haman's estate, and I appoint Mordecai to be the overseer. Poetic justice. Karma is a bitch.

LIFE APPLICATION:

- You reap what you sow.
- Don't be a hater.
- When you don't know what to do, seek counsel. Talk to God about it. Take some time until you have peace about the situation. No rush.

Hannah

(1 Samuel 1:2-2:21)

I really don't want to go to temple this year. It's not that I don't love God; I do. It's just... well, I'm tired of my husband's other wife taunting me because she has tons of kids, and I have none. The one thing I desperately want, I can't have.

My husband loves me more than her. He wipes my tears and tries to console me. He asks me why he isn't enough for me—he's better than ten sons. I agree. He's a wonderful husband, but I want a baby. A son. Not because my culture talks about women who are barren, not so that my sister-wife will shut up (which would be nice), but because everything within me yearns for a child.

I slip away from everyone and go to the altar and pour out my soul. I'm desperate, but all of my groaning is happening inside me. My lips are moving, but no one can hear my anguish—except God. I promise God if he gives me a child, I will bring him back when he is old enough and let him serve in God's house.

Eli, the priest, comes over and accuses me of being drunk because my mouth is moving but no sound is coming out. I explain to him I'm not drunk—I'm just a desperate housewife who wants a child. Eli tells me God has heard my prayer. For the first time since failing to get pregnant all those years ago during our honeymoon, I'm happy. Legit happy.

I go home, eat something, and then have a wild, fun night with my husband.

Guess who's preggers! I name him "Samuel" which means "heard by God" because my prayers were heard by God. I'm very literal.

When he is old enough, I take him back to the temple. I pray over him and give him back to God and Eli. It was hard, but it was the deal I struck. Every year I go see him and take him a new coat. We spend time together, and I see how much he's learning and growing. He's already wise beyond his years.

God blesses me with three more sons and two daughters because I honored my promise to give Samuel back to Him. I miss Samuel, but I know he's in good hands.

Later people seek him out for his wisdom because they know he has a direct line to God. He's very special, and others see that, too. I'm a seriously proud mom.

LIFE APPLICATION:

- Don't give up on your dreams.
- Keep your word to God, to yourself, and to others.

Ruth

(Her own Badass Book in the Bible)

I love my mother-in-law. I'm not just saying that—I really do. She can be a little bitter and depressed at times, but who can blame her? She lost her husband and two sons, one of whom was my husband. That's right—I'm a widow. I'm too young to be a widow, and I'm kind of freaking out. Who is going to take care of us? To make things worse, there's a famine in my homeland where we've living.

Naomi decides to go back to her home country. I'm going with her. There's nothing left for me here, and I've got nothing to lose. Bethlehem sounds intriguing, so why not? I'm down for an adventure. But Naomi doesn't want me to join her. She keeps insisting I stay home. I refuse to listen and tell her that her people will be my people and her God, my God. That seems to convince her—or she just got tired of arguing with me. Either way, I'm going to ~~Disney World~~ Bethlehem! We get to Bethlehem just in time for the barley harvest. Good timing, because we are beyond broke. Naomi's late husband has a wealthy relative, Boaz, who has a large field he's in the middle of harvesting. I follow along behind the pickers and gather up the pieces they drop to take home for Naomi and me to eat. A plant-based diet is all the rage right now, anyway. Boaz sees me and talks to me a little. He's nice, and he's a hottie, so I'm not complaining. Makes a girl feel good. Unbeknownst to me, he tells his workers to intentionally drop barley so that I have more to take home. When I come home with a heavy load of barley, Naomi asks me what's going on. I tell her about meeting this nice man named Boaz. Naomi smiles—I think it's the first time I've seen her smile since her husband and sons died. "Why are you smiling, Naomi? What's going on?" I ask. Naomi tells me Boaz is in the line to marry me. This is a cultural thing—if a son dies, his brother marries the widow. If there's no brother available, you find an uncle or a cousin. You keep going until you find someone to marry the widow. Unfortunately, the widow doesn't get a choice in the matter, but in this case, I don't mind. Boaz is a hunk! And this hunk is going to save us. Naomi tells me Boaz is sleeping in the barn and to go cozy up to him. I think maybe she meant for me to seduce him or something, but that's not really my style. But it could be. It's been a long time since I've been with a man. Bidi bidi bom bom. He wakes up as I sit down at his feet. We start talking and he says that he's pleased I'm taking care of Naomi and being a "worthy woman" instead of only thinking of myself and chasing the hot young guys working in the fields. After that, Boaz goes to speak with the elders, and we get married. He's a good husband, and he truly does save us. Boaz and I have kids, and we have a good life. In fact, my great grandson is David. You know, the kid who killed the giant? The shepherd boy who wrote the 23rd Psalm? Yep, that's my great grandson.

All of this goodness came about because I refused to stay home. I followed Naomi and walked fearlessly into my destiny.

LIFE APPLICATION

- **Follow your gut. Listen to your intuition. It won't let you down.**
- **Never give up.**

The Widow of Zarephath

(1 Kings 17:1-16)

BUT FIRST, SOME BACKGROUND:

Bad King Ahab had pissed off God, so the prophet Elijah declared there would be a famine until God decided otherwise. Then Elijah ran away because he was scared of Ahab. Can't really blame him—I'd totally do the same.

While hiding out, Elijah ran out of food and water. God told him to go to the village of Zarephath and ask a widow to give him some food.

I'm on the outskirts of the village gathering firewood when this crazy homeless man walks up. He asks me for some water in a jug because he's thirsty. Cool. I'm not one to judge, and I can totally do that. But as I start to go get the water, this guy also asks for something to eat, which is a problem.

"Dude, I don't even have a biscuit," I tell him. "I have a handful of flour and a tiny bit of oil in a bottle. I was out here trying to get some firewood so that I could make a last meal for me and my son. After we eat that, we're totally out of food and going to die." No, I'm not a drama queen. It's the truth. Yes, for real. Not the best day ever.

"Don't worry about a thing," he tells me. Easy for him to say. "Go ahead and make me a small biscuit and bring it back here to me. You can make a meal for you & your son after that. I'm Elijah, a prophet of God, and God says your flour and oil won't run out before the famine ends." Well, alrighty then.

I gather my firewood and make him a biscuit. What the hell, have a little faith, right? And damn if that crazy man wasn't right. I go back home, hold my breath, and look in my flour jar. There is still plenty of flour and oil for me and my son to eat! The next day, and the next day, and the day after that, I go to the jar of flour and the jug of oil, and they haven't run out. And they don't until the famine ends. My son and I are still alive, and hey, that's pretty badass.

LIFE APPLICATION:

- Sometimes things don't make sense. Sometimes things look bleak. And sometimes you get an impression or intuition to do or say something. Follow that hunch. It might be the very thing you've been seeking/needing.

- Everything always has been, is now, and always will be fine.
- Trust that anything is 100% possible, 100% of the time.

The Widow of Zarephath

PART 2
(1 Kings 17:17-24)

Yep, me again. Some length of time passes after the whole thing with making Elijah a biscuit. Our bellies are still full, and I'm letting Elijah stay in our loft. See, there's this whole thing about people turning prophets away from their hometowns—basically part of the job description—so he doesn't really have anywhere to go. And I don't want to be the one who kicks God's man out into the streets.

Anyway, things are going well... until today anyway. My son is sick, and now he's stopped breathing.

I'm pissed and I'm scared, and I totally blame Elijah for this. My son is dead, and it's definitely totally his fault. I guess Elijah is pretty upset too. He takes my son from me and goes upstairs to the loft and lays my son on the bed. Then he prays. I'm standing here listening to this prophet, this man of God, and he straight up blames God for my son's death! Asking God why he killed my son, especially after I had opened my home to Elijah. This guy has some *cahones.* Then he asks God to put breath back in the boy. God listens, and my son starts breathing again.

Elijah brings him back downstairs to me and says, "Here's your son. He's alive!"

And I respond, "Now I *truly* believe you're a man of God."

***

Now, I know what you're thinking...

You would think I already know how powerful God and Elijah are—my never-ending flour and oil pretty clearly show that—but there's a difference between knowing and understanding. We understand about a broken leg, but until we've actually suffered a broken leg, we don't KNOW what it's really like to have a broken leg.

When God supplied me with food, I understood him to be God and Elijah to be a godly man. But when God brought my son back to life, I KNEW him as God and KNEW Elijah was a godly man.

Not to mention, when we don't learn a lesson the first time, it's often brought back around to us a second, third, fourth time until we learn it.

LIFE APPLICATION:

- It's okay to question God. He's big enough to handle your questions and your fears.
- Everything always has been, is now, and always will be fine.

- Trust that anything is 100% possible, 100% of the time.

Lydia

(Acts 16:12-15)

I've always considered myself a spiritual and religious woman, and an intelligent one. I've listened to many great people speak through the years—educated men and women talking about all kinds of gods and forms of worship. Ignorance keeps you from the truth, so I try to learn as much as possible. I wasn't born into a Jewish family—in fact, most people where I'm from worship the sun god, Apollo—and I can't put my finger on exactly how I know there's only one God, but somewhere deep in my chest that knowledge just... lives.

I run my own (very successful) business and manage my own home. I don't need a man to help with any of that. I don't need a man to manage my religious worship either. Every Sabbath I meet with a group of women at the river just outside of town to pray together.

This particular Sabbath, these four guys who were passing through town ask if they can join us and share their story. I'm always down to hear a good story, so I welcome them into the group. I wish someone had gotten this all on tape! The story these guys tell—it blows my mind. Being Jewish, I believe there is a Messiah coming, but according to these guys, he's already here! Say what?

As they tell us about him, I feel deep in my chest—in that same place where I know there's only one God—that they're telling the truth. I've never been more sure of anything.

I immediately ask them to baptize me and the rest of my household so we can be true followers of Christ. Then, because I'm a Badass Babe with my own money and nice house, I insist that they come and stay with me. They've given me this precious gift of knowledge, so I want to do something in return—I want to show them some of that good, ol' fashioned Philippian hospitality. I have to beg a little before they agree, but I'm so excited I don't even mind.

Before they leave town, I tell them to spread the word that any believer coming through Philippi is welcome at my house—they'll have a place at my table and a place to lay their heads any time they need one. And in the meantime, I'll keep spreading the good news around Philippi.

LIFE APPLICATION:

- When you know, you know. Believe it when your gut tells you it's right.
- Put your faith in to action.
- Give, and it will be given back to you in ways you can't imagine.
- Hospitality is a gift. Use it to bless others.

Elizabeth

(Luke 1:1-64)

I'm a good person. And I'm not just saying that—righteous and blameless they call me. My husband and I are good Jewish folks, and we follow all of the Lord's commands. But none of that matters. All that matters is whether or not a woman has children, and I don't. Barren. What a terrible word. It makes my mouth dry out and my tongue feel thick when I say it.

My husband, Zechariah, is a priest. You'd think we'd be rewarded for our good works and faithfulness. But now we're old—much too old for having babies—and we've given up hope of ever being parents.

Zechariah comes home from giving offerings at the temple and he's completely mute. What the f—? Like, can't talk at all. At first, I think he's playing some kind of stupid joke on me, but that's not like him. This is for real. I guess life is going to be pretty quiet now.

Then the most unbelievable thing happens... I'm pregnant. It's impossible, but it's true. I'm pregnant! The

42

Lord has shown us favor, hallelujah! Pregnancy does crazy stuff to you, though. A lot of it I expected from hearing the other women in the village talk about it, but there was one thing that came as a total surprise—prophecy. That's right, not only is your girl going to be a momma, but now I'm a prophetess, too. Talk about unusual side effects. I guess pregnancy really *does* affect everyone differently!

My cousin, Mary, comes to visit while I'm secluded during my pregnancy. When she walks in and calls out to me, the baby starts moving like crazy, and I'm gifted with a prophecy. I find myself excitedly responding to Mary, saying, "Why am I so favored that the mother of my Lord should come to me?" Cousin Mary is pregnant too—with the child of God, no less. What are the odds? These are exciting times!

When the baby comes, it's a perfect, beautiful, wriggling, screaming baby boy. And I couldn't be happier! I may be old, but I had this baby like a boss. Eight days later they come to circumcise him, and we announce his name—John. And at the very moment that we name him, Zechariah opens his mouth and begins speaking again!

An angel had come to him to tell him that we were going to have a child, and he doubted. Foolish man. So, he was unable to speak until everything the angel told him about had happened.

My son will grow up to be John the Baptist and do great things, but for now I just hold him in my arms and stare into his perfect face.

LIFE APPLICATION:

- There's no such thing as too late.
- Never give up hope.
- God makes a way when there seems to be no way.

Disruptors

These women went against societal expectations and did what they believed was right or fair.

Some of them disrupted entire countries, and some kept it closer to home,

but God rewarded the strength of all of these Badass Babes.

Shiphrah & Puah

(Exodus 1:15-21)

My girl, Puah, and I are Jewish midwives in Egypt. I'm Shiphrah. I'm sure you've never heard of me, but I'm the midwife who delivered Moses. So, kind of a big deal in retrospect. Anyway, the king of Egypt gets all paranoid and gives orders to Puah and me that all baby boys born to Jewish women are to be killed at birth. Not cool. I mean, who wants to be a baby killer? Not to mention it's totally against our religion, and, let's be honest, we have way more respect for God than for our insecure monarch. Hard pass, your kingliness. But we can't exactly just tell him we're not on board with his baby murder plans, so we pretend we're going to do it and then just... don't.

It's not long before the king figures it out and calls us to the palace. "Shiphrah and Puah," he says in his haughty king voice, "why are you refusing royal orders?" We can't really say, "Because God rules and our king drools." We have to give a somewhat believable answer if we want to keep our jobs... and our heads. But you know how squeamish the men get about this kind of thing, so we go with an answer that won't lead to more questions –"Oh Pharaoh," we say, "Jewish women are just so strong. Their labor is lively and vigorous, and it happens so quickly. They've already had the baby before we can get there!" Darn the luck, right? All the labors have been too fast to get the midwife there, and the baby is hidden by the time we arrive. That's our story, and we're sticking to it.

It's a pretty gutsy move, but it works! Pharaoh dismisses us, heads still attached, and God is pleased with our answer and blesses us with our own families. Totally worth a little civil disobedience.

LIFE APPLICATION:

- **Do the right thing, no matter what.**

Moses' Queen Mum, Hatshepsut

(Exodus 2:1-10)

I'm the heir to my father's throne, but in my country, I can't take the throne unless I'm married or have a son. I have neither, and I have no prospects, so life kinda sucks right now. And now that I'm saying it out loud, what kind of ridiculousness is that? I need a husband to take my own father's throne? That's f'd up.

One day my servants and I go down to the Nile to bathe, and I see something odd in the bushes along the banks of the river. I can't tell what it is from where I'm standing, but whatever it is, it hasn't been there before. Curious (and bored), I send a servant to get it. It's a basket... with a baby inside! What?! A beautiful baby boy just lying in a basket in the river. Wild. No, I haven't been chewing on any coca leaves or 'shrooms.

Where did he come from? He shouldn't be here.

Actually, he should be dead. My dad ordered all of the Jewish baby boys to be killed at birth because he was paranoid that they would overtake his throne. I love my dad, but he's a little cray-cray.

As soon as my servant picks him up, he starts crying. I look around but don't see anyone. Then this teen girl pops up and offers to find a mother to nurse the baby. It's my lucky day! A baby *and* someone to nurse it. I was totally at the right place at the right time. Finders keepers, so I have a baby now! And you know what that means? When dear ol' dad kicks the bucket, I'mma be QUEEN!

That random girl comes through and brings me a nursemaid. I pay her to take the baby home with her so she can nurse him. As it turns out, she's his birth mother, Jochebed. Weird coincidence, right? She had put him in the basket to protect him, hoping someone would find and adopt him. After he is old enough, she brings him back to me to raise in the palace. I name him "Moses," which means "I drew him out of the water." Pretty fitting, if I do say so myself.

Even though I'm the only daughter, and my father's favorite child, I'm afraid to introduce him to my adopted Jewish son because, well, he was supposed to have been killed at birth. Props to Dad, though—he takes it way better than I expect. I happily raise this kid as my own. He lives in the palace and is educated at the best schools. He learns Egyptian and Jewish traditions. He's my son, and I love him. Oh man, do I love this kid. He's taught leadership skills and becomes a man of powerful speech and action—which helps him later in life when he leads his people out of captivity. You may have heard about that "parting the sea" thing... yep, that's my kid. He actually takes on my father and wins. It's bittersweet, for sure. I am *so* proud of him, but I also know I'll never see him again.

Looking back, people say I saved Moses, but really, he saved me. I became queen and, not to brag, but I have one of the most successful Egyptian empires ever. I promote peace (unlike my father). I increase the mining industry and re-establish trade networks. And my success comes because I took care of God's chosen man—my son, Moses, the baby I found in a basket in the river. Who saw that coming?

LIFE APPLICATION:

- You are always right where you need to be.
- Trust the timing.
- The answer you're looking for can come from the most unexpected place.

(Judges 1:11-15)

BUT FIRST, SOME BACKGROUND:

Moses sent spies to Canaan—the Promised Land—to determine whether it could be taken by the Israelites. Only two of the spies, Caleb and Joshua, returned and advised moving troops ahead. As a reward for their faith, the Lord promised that they and their descendants would possess the land.

After years of desert wandering, we've finally "entered the Promised Land" and we're settling the lands in Canaan. My dad, Caleb, led his troops into the city of Hebron. That makes it ours. But it's not quite enough. Dad wants Debir too. It's maybe 15 miles south, and he has crafted quite the plan to get it. He's offering one of his dearest treasures as a reward—me.

You read that right. Dear ol' dad announces to anyone and everyone that I'm up for grabs. This kinda sounds like human trafficking to me. Doesn't he know that *Dateline* will be at his door soon? Whoever is man enough to take

Debir gets to marry me. It's not as bad as it sounds. And he really does treasure me. Obviously, whoever it is will be a strong and fierce warrior, which is a desirable quality in a husband. And I come with a nice piece of land as my dowry. No bag of coins and a necklace that will soon be gone for me. Land will provide us with a steady source of income. I'll grow gardens and have livestock. I don't know of another girl who can claim such a thing. I'm waiting on pins and needles for news of the fall of Debir—and of my husband.

I'm not disappointed. Othniel has returned victorious. He is my father's brother and a fine and brave man; he'll make a good husband. I do have one little bone to pick with my dad though...

I go alone to speak to my father. I don't need my husband to speak for me. I'm no wilting violet or demure lady. I'm going to speak my mind and get what I want. And what I want is some water, dammit! The land is dry as a bone, and that's not gonna fly. There's a field next to our land that has two springs, and it would be perfect!

It's not really a done thing to ask for more like this—improper to impose on the family. But I'm kind of a daddy's girl and have him wrapped around my little finger, so I'm not worried. I'm getting what I want.

LIFE APPLICATION:

- **Don't be afraid to ask for what you need.**
- **Dare to ask for more.**

Woman at the Well

(John 4:4-42)

It's high noon and hot as hell. I really should come to this well in the mornings when it's cooler outside, but I don't want to be around the other women. That's funny. They call *me* "The Other Woman." They're just jealous because men find me attractive, and I'm comfortable in the presence of men. Some would say "too comfortable." It's always a good time for them to mind their own business and keep their damn mouths shut.

Speaking of men, there's a man sitting by the well. Odd. I don't recognize him. He must be a stranger passing through town. I get closer and realize, *Wait. He's a Jew.* This is Samaria. We are sworn enemies. Like Khloe K and Jordyn Woods. Or Tupac & B.I.G. Or Batman and The Joker. Is this guy lost? Or does he have a death wish?

I approach the well, and he asks me for a drink.

"Why are you asking me for a drink? I'm a Samaritan. Our kind don't hang out or do favors for each other."

"If you only knew who's asking you for this drink, you

would have asked him for 'living water.'"

And now I have so many questions... "Why are you talking like a narrator or something? And how're you gonna get a drink? You don't have a cup! And, what's this 'living water' you're talking about? Are you a door-to-door salesman or something? I'm not giving you my credit card. I don't even know you."

"Anyone who drinks this well water keeps getting thirsty. If you drink my water, you'll never get thirsty again."

"Yo, I want some of that! I won't have to keep hauling water from this well. Save my back!"

"Go get your husband and come back."

And there's the rub. Probably one of those guys who thinks women are beneath him and will only talk to the man of the house. Great. "I'm not married."

"You're right, you're not. You've been married five times, but the guy you're currently shacked up with isn't your husband."

Damn, he's got me there. "You, sir, are a prophet! But do you really have to throw shade like that?" He just smiles. I flip him off—in a fun, smartass way.

Now that I know this guy is some kind of Bible nerd, I start asking all sorts of questions about my religion and its history. He patiently answers all of my questions. Then he tells me he is the Messiah (Christ)—the one I've been waiting for. I'm speechless—a first for me.

A bunch of his friends approach him and are surprised he's talking to a woman, especially a Samaritan one. They start quizzing him about why he's there and who I am while totally ignoring me. Now is a good time for me to make my exit.

I leave my jar at the well and head back to town. I tell everyone I see that I've just met the Messiah, and he was able to tell me everything I've ever done. All of the townspeople head to the well to meet this man. I'm not sure what all they talk about, but everyone is getting along so well that they invite him to stay in our town for a while. He stays for two days. So much for The Feud.

All of those women whispered about me behind my back and made nasty comments on my social media stories, but I showed them. Because I'm so bold and can easily talk to men, I met the Messiah. Not only met him, but got some serious one-on-one time with him. Not many people can say that. He changed my life that day. He changed our whole town. Whose sorry now?

LIFE APPLICATION:

- **Talking to strangers isn't always a bad thing. Sometimes you meet someone really cool who changes your life for the better.**
- **When people talk badly about you or judge you, it's a reflection of who THEY are—not who you are. You know your truth.**
- **Don't label people or put them in a box. Once you know their story—their truth—enemies can become BFFs.**

Mary - Mother of Jesus

(Luke 2:1-20; John 2:1-11; Matthew 27:32-56)

I'm fourteen, pregnant, and engaged. If that's not shocking enough, my fiancé isn't the father. In fact, I've never slept with anyone. I'm a virgin and pregnant.

I know what you're thinking. I've heard it all before. I've seen the looks as I walk in the market. I hear the whispers and the giggles. It's quite the scandal, really.

My parents take it surprisingly well. Joseph, my fiancé, is a saint. He has every right to break off the engagement, but he doesn't. What did I do to deserve him?

Fast forward a few months, and I have this poor kid in a stinky stable because there were no hotel rooms available. That's how life started out for him.

He has a normal childhood, but the pressure on me to be raising the son of God?!?! Jesus is my first kid. What do I know about raising a kid—much less the son of God? I know, I keep saying that, but FOR REAL, he's the fricking son of God!

He's a good kid for the most part—except when he runs off to talk scripture with the rabbis. What kid willingly does that? The weird thing is that they actually listen to him. He's only 12, but everyone knows there's something special about him.

He's a carpenter like Joseph, until one day when he puts down the hammer and walks away. He gathers some guys around him that are a pretty rag-tag bunch. I don't even know where he found some of them. He travels around spending all of his time with people most of society doesn't want to be around. It's admirable, I suppose, and the more he travels, the more people start following him and listening to what he has to say.

I don't see him much, with all this traveling he does, but I do get to see him at a friend's wedding. We're all having a great time until the host runs out of wine. It's okay, though—poor planning on his part presents an opportunity for my son to perform his first miracle: turning water in to wine. Everyone is really impressed, and he makes the host look good, too. It's the best wine any of us have ever had!

Everywhere he goes, people flock to him. He's performing more miracles—feeding huge crowds and walking on water. People are being healed: the blind see, the crippled walk, leprosy and COVID are instantly gone. Cities are literally throwing parades for him.

You'd think everyone would be happy, right? Well, you'd be wrong. Those very same rabbis who used to listen to him as a kid and talk with him for hours are now plotting to kill him because he's showing them up. How insecure can you get?

They don't play, and things go from bad to worse. I watch as they go to Pontius Pilate, our governor, and persuade him to have soldiers beat Jesus. I watch them nail him to a cross. I watch them give him vinegar to drink when he's thirsty. I watch him die. And a part of me dies with him.

Even the earth mourns with me. The ground shakes and the sky gets dark. I sit with Mary Magdalene as my son's body is wrapped in linen and prepared for burial in a stone tomb.

Three days later, we return to the tomb with spices to anoint his body, but his tomb is empty! He's alive again! My heart soars and my mind is racing, thankful that I'm about to get more time with my son. But it doesn't last. Forty short days is all we have. He rises into Heaven in a cloud, and I never see him again. But I am forever changed.

LIFE APPLICATION:

- **What others think of you is none of your business.**
- **Encourage and promote your kid's gifts.**
- **Don't be attached to the outcome.**

Mary of Bethany

(Luke 10:38-42)

⟨∾⟩⟨ɞ⟩

My sister is a piece of work, let me tell you. I love her, but everything has to be just so, and perfect, and exactly *how* Martha wants it and *when* Martha wants it. And when we're about to have company is the worst.

I'm a more relaxed, go-with-the-flow kinda girl. Hakuna Matata, man. That's not to say I don't care about anything. I just don't care about everything all the time. It's okay to leave some things for future me to worry about. If I don't get around to dusting today, it'll still be there tomorrow, you know?

It's not like our place is a pigsty. It's neat and tidy, even. So, when we find out Jesus is coming to visit, I'm excited to see our friend. I do the few things that I would have done to straighten up anyway, and then I take my book to the garden. I'm going to chill in the hammock until he gets here, and then the real fun will begin! This guy tells the best stories, and I can listen to him talk for days.

Martha is running around like a crazy person, totally going overboard trying to make everything better-than-perfect. Even after Jesus gets here, she doesn't stop moving and doing and worrying. Me? I just sit at his feet and take in every word. This is what he came for—he came to visit with us, not to eat a perfect dinner in a perfect house.

I know Martha is frustrated, but I do *not* expect what happens next... she straight up snaps on Jesus. "Don't you see Mary left me to do everything? Why don't you tell her to get off her lazy ass and help me?" Damn, sis, take a chill pill.

Jesus isn't having it, though. "Martha, Martha," he says, "you are worried and upset about everything, but only one thing matters right now—the thing Mary has chosen. I'm not going to take that away from her." I could totally gloat, but I don't. Well, maybe, a little.

LIFE APPLICATION:

- Don't let the busyness of your day keep you from the things that should be priorities.
- Everything doesn't have to be perfect. Sometimes "good enough" really is good enough.

Badass Babes of the Bible

Women with a Message

These women had something to say,
and say it they did!

These intelligent and eloquent Badass Babes
spread the messages of God.

Judge Deborah

(Judges 5)

Before Judge Judy, there was Judge Deborah. That's me. My courtroom is under a date palm tree—location, location, location. If you have a dispute, you stand in line and wait your turn to meet me under my tree. I listen to both sides and make a ruling on your matter. I have a reputation for being a fair and honest judge that I'm pretty proud of.

Did I mention that I'm also a prophetess? God tells me things, and I pass the messages on to the people. Pretty cool gig, honestly. And I'm the only female judge mentioned in the Bible. I'll pause here to give you a moment to be appropriately impressed...

The maniacal King Jabin has kept my people, the people of Israel, oppressed for a solid twenty years now. Not cool. Then I get a prophecy—God tells me that my people are to go to war and attack the commander of the King's army, Sisera. I send word to Barak, this kickass military commander, and tell him to gather up

10,000 troops to lead into battle and that God will send Sisera to the river where he can be defeated. Seems like a pretty straightforward plan to me. Then this mighty warrior says, "I'll only go, if you go." Wait, what? You're the mighty warrior. I'm just the messenger, bro. My role as prophetess in this whole shebang is to sing prior to war, not actually go in to battle with the troops. It's like singing the national anthem before a big game. I'm not supposed to put on pads and go for the interception.

But I'm sure you've heard by now that "the Lord works in mysterious ways." Here we go again with one of those mysterious way situations. I finally agree to go, but I give Barak another (unexpected) message—"When we win, you'll get no glory. God will deliver Sisera into a woman's hands." It wasn't Barak's favorite message ever, but he decides it's still worth it to get out from under the rule of King Jabin.

Off to battle we go. Sisera hears that we're coming for him, so he gathers 900 iron chariots and a whole bunch of soldiers. A huge battle rages, and Sisera's army is completely defeated. But remember that caveat about Sisera being killed by a woman? Yeah, so he escapes from the battle on foot. You probably expect that I did it, huh? Sorry to disappoint, but again, I'm just the messenger. It was another Badass Babe who got that honor.

After the battle, the people sing songs about me and how wonderful I am—how embarrassing (but also pretty cool). My reputation increases and, not to brag, but I totally become a very influential leader. Pretty badass, right?

LIFE APPLICATION:

- Women rule!
- A woman can do anything!
- Judge like a girl.

Priscilla

(Acts 18:2-3; Acts 18:26; Romans 16:3)

BUT FIRST, SOME BACKGROUND:

In Greco-Roman society, women were seen as property. They had no free choice and were completely dependent on their fathers and then their husbands. Some members of the early Christian church had a radical (for the time) view of women—that they should be valued and treated as equals. Both men and women were teachers and missionaries for the early church.

My husband, Aquila, and I have been expelled from Rome. Intense, right? I mean, it isn't just us. They didn't bang on our door and escort us to the border or anything. But Emperor Claudius has his knickers in a wad about Christians causing "disturbances" and being "excessively superstitious" so he says we have to GTFO. We're not interested in sticking around to see if Claudius might take a few pages from his Daddy Nero's book on Christian torture, so we peace out.

We travel as far as Corinth in Greece and meet up with one of the original posse—Paul. Like Aquila and I, Paul is a tentmaker by trade, so we pool our resources and live and work together. And on the weekends we go to the synagogue to preach. We help Paul found a church here and have the meetings in our home. Some of the Jews take offense to what we're preaching, though, and they drag Paul to a lawman. When the lawman won't make an arrest on the charge of "persuading people"—yes, seriously... I know—they take him to the square and beat the shit out of him.

We stay in Corinth about 18 months total, but then we decide it's time to dip. Paul keeps traveling, but Aquilas and I settle in Ephesus in Turkey. We continue to preach and share stories of Jesus with the Jews and Gentiles. And I've gotta say, I know my shit. When Paul writes to other missionaries about Aquilas and me, he mentions my name first more often than not. If that doesn't indicate who the badass is, I don't know what does.

This one dude, Apollos, comes rollin' into town and is preaching at the synagogue. He's good, I'll give him that. He talks and people listen. But he's got a few things sideways. We're sitting there listening, and I keep nudging Aquilas. "We've got to set this guy straight," I whisper to him. He nods but does that universal man thing that means, "Shut up, we're not talking about how correct and amazingly smart you are right now." Or, at least, that's what I like to think it means. When Apollos finishes preaching, we invite back to our place and explain a few things.

Narrator in the voice of Lady Whistledown:

Rumor has it that Priscilla is the anonymous author of the Book of Hebrews. It makes sense. She's a smart cookie. Knows her shit. Why shouldn't she write a book? She's a fabulous teacher. If it's true, that makes her the only female to write a book in the Bible. Is the authorship anonymous because it's a Badass Babe author? Or it is that because it was written by a Badass Babe, in order to get it published, the female authorship had to be kept quiet? Time will tell.

LIFE APPLICATION:

- **Women are just as smart and capable as any man.**
- **You are valuable and equal to anyone.**
- **Don't let your gender be an excuse for playing small.**
- **The world needs you.**

Dorcas

(Acts 9:36-42)

BUT FIRST, SOME BACKGROUND:

Not much is known about this Badass Babe. She's only mentioned in part of one chapter in the Bible. It describes how generous she was and how she sewed for others. She gave to the needy, especially widows. The little bit of info we get sounds like she might have been a widow herself, and she probably had money—money that she used to help others. She's also called a follower of Christ—part of the inner circle. Sounds like a pretty wonderful person. A kind and selfless Badass Babe, for sure!

My story starts in an unlikely place—with my death. I know, weird place to start because it sounds like the end, but trust me, this is going places...

So, I get sick and die. Not to gloat, but this is an absolute tragedy, and everyone in my community is totally devastated. I mean, what can I say? I help people around here a lot, and everyone likes me. My friends wrap my body and leave... it? Me?... in a cool room. Because that's what we do. You know, so I won't rot too fast. Gross. Somebody get some room spray and light some scented candles.

Peter—one of Jesus' posse and a pretty important dude—is in a nearby town, so one of my friends sends for him. Again, not to brag, but I'm pretty important and well-respected, so he comes immediately.

When Peter arrives, the widows gather around him, showing him all of the beautiful things I've made for them. They are obviously upset and wailing over the loss of their friend. He can't handle the tears and tells everyone to leave the room. Typical man.

But I'll forgive him because of what happens next. He kneels down beside my body, prays, and then speaks to me. "Dorcas," he says, "get up."

And it works. I open my eyes and look at Peter. Literally raised from the dead. If that doesn't qualify for Badass Babe status, I don't know what does. He takes my hand and helps me up. Then he calls everyone back in the house and presents a now-alive me to them. Kind of embarrassing. Like, sorry for the drama guys, but I was just kidding about being dead... Anyway, the place goes nuts! Which is understandable as it was a freaking miracle. Then word spreads about what happened, and because of little ol' me, people start believing in Jesus. How was your day? But did you die?

LIFE APPLICATION:

- **Be faithful in the "small" things.**

- You don't have to do great things to make an impact.
- Use your gifts and talents to serve others.

Prophetess Anna

(Luke 2:36-38)

BUT FIRST, SOME BACKGROUND:

Old Testament law requires that all families take their newborn babies to the Temple to make a purification offering and present the child to the Lord. When Jesus was 40 days old, Mary and Joseph took him to the Temple in Jerusalem to make their offering.

People may think I'm a little eccentric, but they listen when I speak. They kind of have to—I'm a prophetess, so the Lord speaks through me. No one wants to miss anything the big guy has to say! But I never leave the Temple, so that's probably a little weird. It's like if you turned the janitor's closet at work into your bedroom. Total workaholic. But where else would I go? What else would I do?

I was married once upon a time—happily married for seven years. Then I became a widow. We had no children, so I devoted my life to the Lord and my work in the

Temple. That was a long time ago—eighty-four years, actually—so you best believe I've seen some messed-up shit.

Today takes the cake, though. I'm chillin' at the Temple, doing my thing, fasting and praying and whatnot, when I hear voices. Not *that* kind of voices. Actual voices. People are coming into the Temple, and it sounds like they have a baby with them. I better go check it out.

As I step into the room, I'm overcome with joy, filled with light. I give thanks to the Lord, praising Him because... are you ready for this? Our Redeemer is here! This baby is the one we've been waiting for. He's the one who will save us all.

I have no time to waste. I have to share this prophecy, the significance of this child, with everyone in Jerusalem who needs to hear it.

LIFE APPLICATION:

- When you have good news, tell everyone who needs to hear it. Spread your joy!
- What I desire, desires me.
- You're never too old or too young to pursue your dreams and live out your purpose.

Phoebe

(Romans 16:1-2)

BUT FIRST, SOME BACKGROUND:

After the murder of Jesus, his disciples and many of his followers became missionaries—taking the teachings of Jesus out to different communities across the northern part of the Mediterranean Sea. Jews and Gentiles (non-Jews) were converting to Christianity in Greece and Italy. Paul, one of the disciples, traveled across the Roman Empire covering 10,000 miles over thirty years. He preached in homes and synagogues, but there was no Bible in those days to explain central beliefs and unify believers. There was a lot of in-fighting and arguing over how things should be done. On top of that, the Roman government and Emperor Nero led a campaign of persecution against Christians making it incredibly dangerous to be a believer.

I know this is going to sound dramatic, but life is so hard. I'm proud of what I've accomplished and what I'm doing, but with that is always an undercurrent of fear and, if I'm honest, exhaustion. Some days it's so tempting to give up. But I keep going because deep down I know that what I'm doing is important. The message of Christianity is one everyone needs to hear, and the thought of all the people who haven't heard it yet keeps me going.

And it's not like I can sit at home in my yoga pants and post this stuff on TikTok. I have to *go*. I have to be where the people are. (Anyone else get mermaid vibes there? Just me?) These people can be a little much sometimes, though. At first all of the converts were Jewish—which makes sense because Jesus was Jewish—but lately Paul has been preaching to the Gentiles, too. I'm totally on board with leaving no man behind, but it's creating some chaos. The formerly-Jewish still want to hold onto all of their customs and make them part of Christianity. The Gentiles are pushing back on that, and everyone is pissed at someone else. Not only are these jokers fighting with each other, but they're being persecuted by the Romans, who are spreading these crazy stories about how we're all incestuous cannibals or some such bullshit. Believers are being arrested and tortured and publicly executed. And I'm not talking a quick "off with their heads!" Some are being crucified, some are being thrown to wild animals, and some are being burned alive. You'd think we're witches or something.

There isn't much we can do about the persecution aside from keep our heads down and avoid attention from the wrong people, but Paul says he has a solution to the in-fighting in Rome—he's going to write them a letter. We'll see if that works. Better be some spectacular writing! In fact, I'll see first-hand, as yours truly has been tapped to be the messenger. I know I sound kind of 'whatever' about it, but I'm just playing it cool. It's actually a super big deal. I'm kind of a big deal. Paul even wrote a letter of introduction for me explaining that I'm his representative and a deacon—the only woman in the whole Bible given that title. Pretty badass. I'm setting off on a journey from Corinth to Rome, and I'll do some preaching on the way. Keep your fingers crossed I stay in one (non-crispy) piece.

LIFE APPLICATION:

- Women can do anything and belong everywhere.
- Words matter. They create fights or peace. It's a choice. Choose wisely.
- Ultimately, nothing and no one can keep you from something you truly believe in.
- When you're entrusted with something, follow through with it all the way to completion. Even if it's inconvenient. No excuses.
- Be 100% responsible for your actions.

Women Who Stood Strong in Adversity

These Badass Babes really got the shit end of the stick in life.

Despite some truly horrible things happening to them, they stood strong and faced their adversity with grace.

Badass Babes of the Bible

Tamar

(Genesis 28:6-30)

BUT FIRST, SOME BACKGROUND:

*The television show The Crown has nothing on this royal family.
Rape, betrayal, murder... it's all here.*

*Amnon is madly in love with his half-sister Tamar. He wants
her so badly that he and his friend, Jonadab, devise a plan so
that he can have Tamar. The plan is to tell his father, King
David, that he feels very ill and would like for Tamar to bring
him some food because that's the only thing that will make him
feel better. (Seriously? That's the best he can come up with?)
David doesn't know Amnon has ulterior motives and agrees to
allow Tamar to visit Amnon.*

As a daughter of King David, I grow up in the palace.
Trust me, it's not as glamorous as it sounds. I'm fifteen and
not married yet, so I'm kept in seclusion (gotta protect
that virginity, you know). I'm only allowed to venture out
if I have people with me to be witnesses to whatever I do.
It's a system that works... until it doesn't.

So, I have this half-brother... actually I have a lot of half-siblings. Dear old dad has more kids than he has fingers and toes. But this one in particular, Amnon, he's a real douchebag. He tells dad that he doesn't feel well, and he asks if I can bring him something to eat. Dad knows a bunch of servants will be around, so he sends me to Amnon's chambers without a chaperone. No big deal.

I make him a biscuit, as requested. He refuses to eat it and says he'll only eat if I feed it to him. I don't want to, but I want to get out of here. So, I feed him the stupid biscuit. I should just shove it in his mouth. Then he sends the witnesses away. My danger-o-meter is off the charts, and I am legitimately scared now. He tells me that he's madly in love with me, and how badly he wants me, and what he is going to do to me. I am not prepared for this conversation. At all.

I'm terrified. I beg him to not be a fool. All he has to do is ask our father for me, and he'll have us get married and everything can be above board. (I know—half-siblings marrying is icky, but it's totally a normal thing for us. Seriously.)

Amnon doesn't care about doing the right thing and asking for me. He's determined to have me immediately. I try to fight him off, but he's too strong. He rapes me. Once he's done, he's overcome with guilt and shame. He turns on me and has hate in his eyes. I can see it clearly— he absolutely despises the sight of me. I beg him not to send me away. I'm spoiled goods now. No one will have me. If Amnon doesn't marry me, I'll never be a wife or mother. He doesn't care. He got what he wanted.

I can't stay at the palace. Another of my brothers,

Absalom—a good brother—takes me in. I tell him what happened, and, man, is he pissed. Murderously angry. Literally. Two years after I move in with him, he murders Amnon. Sorry, not sorry. This is my life now. I'll live out my days on my brother's generosity. I'll never marry or have a family. But neither will Amnon, and I guess that's something.

LIFE APPLICATION:

- Speak your truth.
- Trust your gut!
- Don't take on guilt or shame that aren't yours.
- A traumatic event doesn't have to define your or keep you in hiding—or be your excuse. You may be the innocent recipient of some horrible event, but you don't have to be a victim.

Jochebed

(Exodus 2:1-10)

How many women get paid to nurse their own babies? Weird question, right? But I do. My beautiful, strong, perfect baby boy. And it's the most bittersweet, emotionally painful thing I can imagine because I know I can't keep him.

I have to give him away, and soon. I shouldn't have had him this long. See, we're Jewish and living in Egypt. The pharaoh has decreed that all sons born to Jewish women must be killed at birth, but Shiphrah, my midwife, just couldn't bring herself to do it.

I'm thankful to her, but that also puts us in a lot of danger. Instead of showing him off to my friends, I have to hide him. It's for his protection—and mine. I don't want to be without him, but the jig is up.

My daughter, Miriam, and I put the baby in a basket by the river where the pharaoh's daughter would find him. She wants to raise him, so she is paying me to nurse him and then bring him back to her when he's weaned. And now it's that time. Time to drop him off.

It's the hardest thing I've ever done. It's the best thing that could happen for him.

My life will never be the same. I know that giving him up will create a hole in my heart that will never heal. And his life will be completely different.

He'll be raised in a different culture—our captor's culture. He'll be taught and loved and cared for by the same people who keep his mother and his siblings oppressed. He might never know that. I can't imagine. He will have the best of everything while we struggle to have enough. He'll never have to work a day in his life while we slave away at hard labor.

Why did I make this deal in the first place? Because I want him to live and to prosper.

I know there's something special about him. I want him to have every possible advantage in life.

I make sure his new mother has his favorite teddy bear and blanket. I kiss him one last time and walk out the door, tears rolling down my face. I don't look back.

LIFE APPLICATION:

- **Love is a verb.**
- **Do what's in the best interest of your child.**

Leah

(Genesis 29-30)

BUT FIRST, SOME BACKGROUND:

Jacob is on the run from his brother, Esau, who wants to kill him because Jacob stole his birthright (with the help of their misguided mom, Rebekah). Talk about dysfunctional family!

Jacob ends up at a well in the middle of nowhere. He talks to the shepherds who tell him that Laban owns the land and the sheep. About this time, a smokin' hot young lady enters the picture. She is the shepherdess of these sheep and Laban's daughter, Rachel. Jacob immediately helps her with the sheep, waters them, and then KISSES her and bursts into tears. This boy is in love.

He tells Rachel they're cousins, and she runs to tell her dad, Laban, that Jacob is in the 'hood. Laban comes out to meet Jacob and welcome him as family.

*Jacob has been working for Laban for a month when Laban tells Jacob he can't work for free just because he's family. He asks Jacob how he can pay him. Jacob takes the opportunity to ask to marry Rachel. He even says he'll work SEVEN years for her. Man does he have it bad! Laban agrees. Jacob works seven years to marry Rachel, but it "seemed like only a few days" because Jacob loved her so much. *Heavy sigh**

At the end of the seven years, Jacob is ready to get married. Laban throws a big party. And here's where the story goes sideways:

Laban switches out his daughters. He sends in his older daughter, Leah, to sleep with Jacob and consummate the marriage. Allegedly, Jacob didn't notice it wasn't Rachel until the next morning—was he that drunk? Seriously?

Anyway, Jacob is understandably pretty pissed, and he confronts Laban saying he's been cheated. Laban says he can't let his younger daughter marry first—that's not the tradition. Laban brushes Jacob off and tells him to enjoy his honeymoon week. Then, if he still wants to marry Rachel, he totally can. He just has to work ANOTHER SEVEN YEARS to pay off the debt for her. The audacity! But Jacob agrees. After his honeymoon week with Leah, he takes Rachel as his wife and sleeps with her. Slap. In. Leah's. Face.

My husband doesn't love me. He's in love with my younger sister. And thanks to our dad, he's married to both of us. Yes, we have a jacked-up family.

My divine consolation is that I easily get pregnant—a real fertile Myrtle—and my sister can't. Honestly, though, I think I'd prefer to have Jacob's love.

One day my oldest son comes home from the field with mandrakes. They're aphrodisiacs and thought to have fertility power, so of course, Rachel wants them. That pisses me off. How dare she! First, she gets my husband, and now she wants my son's mandrakes! I fume for a bit, and then I offer to make a deal with Rachel: I'll trade her the mandrakes for a night with Jacob. Rachel agrees. What?! I totally wouldn't have done it if I were her, but I'm not complaining.

Jacob gets home from work, and I greet him with "You're mine tonight." Sure enough, that night I get pregnant with son number five. Then I have another son—still hoping it will make Jacob love me. The sixth time isn't the charm either. Then I have a daughter. Maybe now he will love me.

He doesn't. He never did. He only wants Rachel, Rachel, Rachel. That's all I ever hear.

But despite being "Leah the Unloved"—what a depressing identifier—I don't regret my place in the big picture. I may not have had Jacob's love, but I'm mother to six of the twelve nations of Israel. And that's not nothing.

LIFE APPLICATION:

- God never overlooks anyone.
- Love yourself.
- You are enough.
- Not everyone will like or love you, and that's ok.

Rachel

(Genesis 29-30)

I'm sharing my husband with my sister, Leah. No, this isn't a *Sister Wives* episode. He loves me, not her. I know—they all say that. But he agreed to work for my father for fourteen years to have me. She's just the baby maker. I have no children. Clearly, it's my fault. What's wrong with me? I just want *one*. Desperately. Just one would be enough to fill this hole in my heart.

Each time I bleed, I cry. Another failed attempt at becoming a mother. I look out and see her and her kids playing and eating around the tent, having fun together. They are my nephews and niece, and I really do love them, but they also make my despair almost overwhelming. It drives a knife into my heart every single time I see them. I don't know how much longer I can keep going. I feel like I'm being held together with the thinnest of strings, and any moment I'm going to shatter into a million pieces.

My only consolation is that Jacob, our husband, comes home to me, not her.

How did it come to this? Leah and I were close as kids. Our father created this mess by deceiving Jacob. Jacob thought he was marrying me, but it was Leah he married. I felt for Leah at first, I really did—until she started spitting out all these boys. Now it feels like it's her way of getting revenge on me. At this point, I'm so desperate for a child that I let Jacob sleep with my personal assistant, and she becomes a surrogate for us. Stupid. But I get two sons to raise. I love them, but it's not the same. I'm still completely desperate for a child of my own.

For a brief period of time, Leah isn't able to conceive. I silently gloat. I know, that's terrible, but do you really blame me?

There's this plant called the mandrake, and it's believed to be an aphrodisiac and promote fertility. We both want some. Leah's son brings some home, and Leah and I fight over it.

Leah says to me, "You already have my husband. Now you want my mandrakes, too?" Did I stutter? Yes, bitch, that's exactly what I want!

I so desperately want this fertility plant that I trade one night with Jacob for the plant. And, of course, Leah gets pregnant AGAIN. Seriously? FML.

Finally, the Lord has mercy on me and grants me a child. Ultimately, I have two sons, and one of them even becomes famous for his coat of many colors.

All of those painful years of longing were worth it when I finally held my sons in my arms.

LIFE APPLICATION:

- Never give up on your dreams.
- Jealousy makes you do stupid things.

Hagar

(Genesis 16 and 21)

Sarah, my boss, is making me sleep with her husband. He's old and gross, but I do what I'm told because that's what servants do—they appease their masters. And my master wants a baby. Seems that her God told her husband he would be father, but she's like 90 or 100 or something. She can't conceive, so apparently that makes me the obvious solution. Whatever. I don't get a choice; I do as commanded.

I get pregnant, and she goes ape shit. Turns into an absolute psycho bitch. Make up your mind, woman! I did what you said. Produced what you wanted. Now, chill the f— out.

She doesn't. She makes my life completely miserable. She's constantly complaining to Abraham and treating me horribly. Finally, I can't take it anymore, so I run away to the desert. Yes, the desert is better than this place.

In the desert, an angel approaches me. Is it a mirage? Am I having a heat stroke? He tells me to go back to

Sarah. Not this shit again. The angel tells me to name my son Ishmael. He also tells me my son is going to be a troublemaker and won't get along with anyone. He literally says my kid will be "a wild ass of a man." Great. First, Sarah. Now, my son. Geez, Louise. Can't a girl catch a break?

I go back to Abe & Sarah's place like the angel instructed, because if I know anything, it's how to obey. I also know God saw me in the desert. He has my back, and that gives me the strength and confidence to go back. I really don't want any trouble with anyone. I just want to have this baby and get on with my life. Maybe Sarah will leave me alone when this kid is born.

I name him Ishmael. Things roll along pretty much as expected for several years. Then Sarah has a kid. I have mixed feelings about this. Part of me is a little bitter because this means everything Sarah put me through was totally unnecessary, but part of me celebrates hoping this means Sarah will finally chill the hell out.

Yeah, no. Nothing is ever that easy. My son, as predicted, is a troublemaker. One day Sarah hears him making fun of her precious baby Isaac, and that was it. She couldn't bear the thought of her son sharing his inheritance with my son, so she demanded we leave. Abe didn't stand up to her or for my son, but he did pack us a lunch before sending us in to the wilderness. What a guy.

We are homeless now. We wander around the desert aimlessly because I don't know the area. I don't have any family in this country, and I don't know what to do. Our water runs out. Despair creeps in. I put Ishmael under a tree to shade him, and I walk away. I can't bear to watch him die. I find a place out of his sight and hearing and begin to cry. It's been a tough few years. Everything comes rising to the surface. I can't control it or stuff it down anymore.

"Why are you crying, Hagar?" a voice says to me. It sounds familiar. It's the same angel as before! "Don't be afraid. God sees you and Ishmael. He's got you. Ishmael's going to be father to a great nation. Now, go get him, and get out of here."

Well, alrighty then. I wipe my eyes and look up. There's a well. That well wasn't there before, I promise! I fill our water bottle and make sure Ishmael gets a drink. And we all live happily ever after, the end. I wish.

Like I said, nothing is ever that easy. We do lively peacefully for a while, though. Ishmael grows up and becomes a great archer. I find him a nice Egyptian wife and they have a son. Life is good.

But the prophecy eventually comes true. My son can't get along with anyone—a wild ass of a man, indeed. You know all of the trouble in the Middle East? Yeah, that's thanks to my boy! The Arab nation is descended from him. Everyone here fights over land and religion. The Islam religion and Muslims are descendants of my son. What a legacy.

LIFE APPLICATION:

- **God sees you—not in a spooky, creepy, or vindictive way. He hasn't forgotten you. He has your back.**

- Even when people fail you, God won't.

Mary Magdalene

(Luke 8:1-3; Mark 15:37-16:7; John 20:11-18)

They say we're lovers. We're closer than that, but it's pure and spiritual, not shameful or physical. We're soulmates. I understand him and his mission, his teachings, better than the other disciples.

I owe my life to him, really, so there's another layer of connection we have that the others don't. I was possessed by seven demons. Seven! He cast them out and the torment is gone. I'm no longer the crazy demon lady. Now you understand why I owe him my life. I owe him everything.

They say we're secretly married. They say I was a prostitute. They say I have ulterior motives. They say a lot of stupid shit.

They say he hangs around me because I have money, but that's not the reason. No, he feels safe with me. He trusts me.

Trust.

That's something I used to struggle with. What are people's motives? Who is this Jesus dude? Is he for real?

Oh, he's for real. I knew it the moment the demons departed my body. After that, I never wanted to be far from him. Is it out of fear the demons might come back? Or is it because of the gratitude I feel? Or is it the love that exudes from him? Yes, yes, and yes. He's pure, unadulterated love. He never condemned me for having demons. He only loved me. He brought me into his circle, into his confidence. He gave me a place among the people most important to him.

People can talk all they want. I know what he did for me. He set me free.

LIFE APPLICATION:

- People are always gonna talk. Ignore them.
- It's always a good time to mind your own business.
- Jesus is trustworthy.
- God doesn't hold your past against you. He releases you from it.

Badass Babes of the Bible

Women Who Repented

These women were human
and made mistakes
just like the rest of us.
But God can forgive anything,
and these Badass Babes
changed their ways.

She Got Caught

(John 8:1-11)

The first slivers of dawn light seep into my room. I stretch out my arm and realize I'm alone in my bed. I didn't start that way. The guy I was with last night must have slipped out to go home to his wife after I fell asleep. Loser.

I hear a noise and open my eyes. I'm not alone after all, and my chest gets tight with fear. What is this? Why are these men in my bedroom? Where are they taking me? *Let go of me! Someone help me!*

I'm scared. A group of men—religious leaders—are dragging me out of my house. I don't know where I'm being taken. I don't know why. I don't understand what's going on. I struggle and try to get away, but there are too many of them and they're too strong. *Stop pulling on me! You freaks!*

Up ahead I see a crowd in the temple courts. They push me in front of the crowd.

"Hey, Jesus! This woman was caught in the act of

adultery," they yell.

Thanks for putting my business out there. Hey, wait. Adultery takes two. Where's he? Why isn't he being dragged out here?

"The law says she's to be stoned to death. What do you say about that, Jesus?"

What are these men up to? This isn't about me at all. It's about Jesus. They're setting him up. They're worse than I thought. Don't fall for it, Jesus!

The crowd is yelling and pushing all around me. Jesus stoops down and starts writing in the dust. I can't see what he's writing. Is that a name? I think I recognize that name as one of the jerks that dragged me over here. I can't read his writing very well, but it looks like he might be guilty of the same thing I did. Jesus keeps writing, ignoring the crowd.

They keep demanding an answer. Jesus finally stands up and says, "Okay, I'll give you an answer. But first, I want to know which one of you is without sin so that you can throw the first stone." Then he bends back down and continues writing in the dust.

Suddenly, it's quiet. I look around. It's just me and Jesus. He looks at me and asks where my accusers are. I shrug. Beats me.

"Looks like no one is here to condemn you. I don't condemn you, either. Go home and do better."

My life is instantly changed. No more hiding. No more clandestine encounters. No more married men. No more shame or condemnation. I go home and do better.

LIFE APPLICATION:

- We don't have to walk around in shame for choices we've made.
- Shame thrives in darkness and silence. Once it's brought into the open, it no longer has power over us.
- Love yourself enough to change. We can tell a different story about ourselves starting now.
- You are enough.

Martha

(Luke 10:38-42)

Type A

Driver/Driver

Hustle!

Work until your eyes bleed.

10X.

More action, less talk.

That's me! I stay busy doing all of the things. My house is immaculate—there's a place for everything, and everything is in its place. My hair and makeup are on pointe. It's going to be a good day.

Jesus is stopping by today. This place needs to be spotless. My sister, Mary should be helping, but *wait, where's Mary? Oh, there she is—sitting outside in the hammock reading a book.* Seriously?

I start to yell at her, but what's the point? She's useless. Her head is always in the clouds. Better to just do everything myself. At least then I know it's done right.

There's a knock at the door. It's him! I welcome him in and start rushing around making sure he's comfortable, that his feet are washed, that he has the best pillow. I'm passing out hors d'ouevres, checking to make sure the bread isn't burning and the meat isn't drying out, opening the wine, pouring and serving the glasses, getting refills, checking on dessert, and... I stop in my tracks.

"What's that, Jesus? I need to be more like Mary?"

I'm stunned. Are you f'ing kidding me right now??? He can't be serious. WTF. I just did ALL of this for him. Doesn't he see how hard I work and how much effort I put in? Doesn't he know Mary did *nothing*? Absolutely not a damn thing. Left it all for me to do, per usual.

He'd rather I ... what? Sit? Be still? Is he smoking crack? Nothing gets done if everyone is just sitting around! And there are things that have to be done... so many things.

"What's that? It's better to be still? Were you already drinking before you got here? Don't you appreciate the lengths I've gone to trying to impress you?" I must be in an alternate universe. I've fallen through the looking glass.

And then... "I don't need to impress you? You still love me?"

I don't have to DO anything to be loved? That doesn't sound right. I can just sit here, be still, quiet my mind and heart, and... that's it? That's enough? I don't have to do anything to earn your love?

That seems too easy.

Let it be easy.

LIFE APPLICATION:

- Be still and know.
- Allow. Trust. Surrender.
- Let it be easy.
- You are enough. You don't have to earn anyone's love.

Miriam

(Exodus 2:1-10; Exodus 15:20-21)

I saved my brother's life when he was a baby. In fact, my brother, Moses, got to live in a palace most of his life thanks to me. No big deal. I lived at home with my other brother, Aaron. We didn't see Moses at all as we were growing up. Now, he's going against the Pharaoh and leading our people out of captivity and towards the Promised Land. And I'm helping him do that. I sing songs and dance, and as Moses parts the Red Sea for us, I lead the women across. I have to admit, the whole sea thing is hands-down the coolest thing ever!

After escaping from the Pharaoh's army, we roam in the wilderness for 40 years. Moses is the "Chosen One" and leads the people, but Aaron and I help Moses lead and provide counseling. I love the people, and they love me. Life is definitely not what I expected, but it's good.

Moses gets married, and I don't like his wife. He also marries a second woman who is from another country and doesn't share our religion. I don't know what he's thinking, but I call him out on it. He may be the boss, but I know he's definitely not perfect. And I have no problem letting him know it. Just being a good sister, ya know?

Besides, Moses always gets everything he wants. He was raised in a palace, has two beautiful wives, and is the chosen one to lead us to the Promised Land, but he's not all that. He actually divorces his first wife. That's a huge no-no. I call him out on that, too.

Aaron and I didn't grow up in a palace. We didn't get the education he did. But here we are, all doing the same job, with Moses getting all the credit. And the title.

The people are getting tired of walking around the same mountain year after year. I get it—I'm ready to leave the desert too—but, man, they are a bunch of complainers. Totally getting on my nerves. They're always whining about something and blaming everyone else, especially Moses. They whine about eating the same food every day. So, God gives us something special to eat. Pretty cool, right? You'd think that would placate them for a while. Nope. They get tired of that pretty quickly and whine some more. I love these people, but they're seriously annoying. It doesn't help that Moses isn't doing much to stop them. He just keeps caving into their demands and enabling their bad behavior.

I seriously can't take this anymore. Their whining, my own popularity, and Moses' inability to make them stop complaining have finally driven me to do something. It's time to talk to Aaron.

I go to Aaron in secret and we have a little pow-wow. I mean, the best leadership comes from listening to more than one voice, right? Aaron and I have done enough for Moses and for the people that we should be getting a say in things by now. Has the Lord really only spoken through Moses? I don't think so. He's totally spoken through me and Aaron too. I tell Aaron exactly that, and he agrees with me! Smart guy. I'm able to convince Aaron to stand up to Moses with me—after all, we've been leading all these people for the past forty years, too!

I certainly don't expect what comes next. Our standing up to Moses doesn't go over too well. I'm struck with leprosy. I turn snow white—but without the dwarves. Aaron and Moses both appeal to God on my behalf, but I'm banned from the camp for seven days because I'm unclean. No one can come near me. And the real kick in the ass? Nothing happens to Aaron. Not a damn thing. Just me. Why just me? Doesn't seem fair, does it?

But I have seven days to sit here and think about EVERYTHING.

Seven days to reflect on what I did.

Seven days to sit alone in isolation and silence.

Seven. The number of completion and perfection.

That's a lot of time to think about what I've done.

And at the end of those seven days, I've realized a few things about myself that I'm not proud of. I'm 100% responsible for my actions. It wasn't the people's fault or Moses' fault. I bought in to my own hype. I lived for the likes and heart emojis. I had 2 million followers. I was an influencer before that was a thing. People waited for my posts and wanted to read my comments. I was a life coach, motivational speaker, and spirit guide. I sang the songs of the people centuries before Billie Eilish. I was Oprah, Maya Angelou, Judge Judy, Kim Kardashian, and Alicia Keyes all rolled in to one.

I was also jealous and full of myself. And that led to my sitting here contemplating my life.

The people welcome me back into the camp, but things are never quite the same. I've changed; I don't talk much. I don't seek recognition or the spotlight. It just seems so unimportant now, you know? I make peace with God, with Moses, and with the people, but unfortunately, I don't make it to the Promised Land.

A year before our people entered the promised land, I died and was buried in Kadesh. It sucks, but when I died, the well suddenly dried up, and the rock from which water used to flow IN THE DESERT disappeared. I think that qualifies me as a definite Badass!

LIFE APPLICATION:

- **Actions have consequences.**
- **Silence and reflection bring clarity of thought. The answers you seek are within you.**

Misguided Babes

These Badass Babes were, well... bad.

Misguided, we like to say.

They had passion, loyalty,

and determination that can be

admired, but they didn't use

their powers for good.

Even so, they still have lessons to teach us.

Badass Babes of the Bible

(Genesis 1-4)

You think being the first woman in space is a big deal? Try being the first woman on Earth. That's pretty Badass if I do say so myself—makes me want to do my hair toss and check my nails, if you know what I mean. At first, everything was perfect. It was just me, Adam, and the animals. The weather was perfect. The animals were cute, fun, and perfect. The garden was perfect. The food was perfect. Adam was perfect. Our lives were perfect. Maybe that's why I took a bite of the forbidden fruit. Maybe that's why I let that snake tempt me. Everything was perfect. Too perfect.

It wasn't my fault, really. The devil snake tricked me. Adam was standing there right beside me when I took the first bite. He had the second bite, but does anyone talk about that? NOOOO. It's all me. I'm the reason for the fall of humanity. I'm the reason woman have to go through painful childbirth. I'm the reason men have to work. I'm the reason there's death. It's all my fault. I should change my name and go into witness protection.

I guess that's basically what God did for us. He clothed us and moved us out of the Garden of Eden. Life was never the same again. We had bad weather and deserts. We fought. We made up. We had kids. They fought. One son killed his brother and lied about it. Oy vey. We really were the first dysfunctional family.

God was still with us and loved us, but life and the world were never the same.

LIFE APPLICATION:

- **Be 100% responsible for your actions.**
- **Actions have consequences.**
- **Run from temptation. Don't entertain it for a second. It's not worth it.**

Bathsheba

(2 Samuel 11)

Let me set the scene here... My husband, Uriah, is a commander in the King's army and away at war. I'm home alone (well, except for my servants, obviously) and it's a beautiful night. I decide to take a bath on my rooftop—I know it sounds weird, but it's a common thing, I promise. So, I'm up there, enjoying my bath in the moonlight. I didn't really think about whether anyone could see me up there, and I had NO idea I was being spied on. The next thing I know, I'm "summoned" (that's polite-speak for "taken whether I want to go or not") to King David's palace. He tells me that he's been watching me bathe. Yikes. And, you can't exactly say no to the king, so when he makes moves, I have to go along with it. Yes, we have sex. And then, booty call complete, he sends me back home. Classy guy.

I try not to think about it, but then I don't bleed for weeks. I send word to the king that I'm pregnant with his baby. Oops. The next thing I know, my husband is called back from battle. That's highly unusual and definitely more than a little sus. But Uriah is nothing if not a man of principle. He refuses to stay in the house with me because he feels guilty knowing he should be with his men in battle. Turns out King David was hoping we'd celebrate our reunion by getting busy, and then I could pass off the baby as Uriah's. When that plan fails, David sends him back into battle. But not just back into battle—Uriah's regiment is sent to the front lines to be cannon fodder. No chance of survival. And thanks to David, I am now a widow.

But I am also carrying his child.

David "does the right thing" and marries me. Lucky wife number seven. He's older now and not as handsome as he once was. He may be favored by God, but he obviously has his flaws. I mean, he had my husband killed to hide the fact he slept with me while my husband was at war—where, by the way, David should have been, too. Then our baby dies seven days after his birth. David thinks he's consoling me by sleeping with me. Men, am I right? Then he trades me in for a younger woman who becomes wife number eight. Not gonna lie, this story kinda sucks so far.

But it gets better! David manipulated my life... now it's my turn. I go back to David's bed and get pregnant again. I have another son, Solomon. (You may have heard of him—super wise, did the whole "cut the baby in half" trick.) Now, Solomon is not in line for the throne—his half-brother Adonijah is—but I don't care. I want him to be king, and I'm determined to make it happen. I bide my time, playing the good wife and mother. I can be patient when I want to be. When it's clear that David is on his deathbed and Adonijah is about to become king, I put my plan into action. I conspire with David's trusted advisor, and together we get rid of the competition. David anoints Solomon as king. And as an added bonus, I'm now the Queen Mother and help advise my son on various kingdom matters. Take that. I'm one of the most powerful people in the country now, and one of only five women listed in Jesus' ancestry. Not bad.

Real Housewife of Jerusalem: You may have played me, but I ultimately played you. Queen Mother, Bitches.

LIFE APPLICATION:

- Your past doesn't determine your future.
- Anything and anyone can be used for good.
- Everything has been, is now, and always will be fine.

Gomer

(Hosea 1-3)

I'm a prostitute. My husband, Hosea, is a famous preacher dude. Opposites attract, right? Not so much, actually. He loves me. I feel pretty 'meh' about the whole thing. He says God told him to marry me. Whatever.

We have three kids. Maybe they're his, maybe not. I don't know, and he doesn't seem to care. Honestly, I don't want to be a mom. I want to have fun and be treated special, so I keep turning tricks. It's a pretty risky business, though. If I get caught, I'll be stoned—and not with drugs. With actual rocks. Stoned to death. Still, it's not enough of a deterrent.

I leave Hosea and the kids. After a while, God tells Hosea to come and get me. He rolls up while I'm with a customer, and he pays my customer to get me back. Seriously? It's embarrassing. And annoying. And kind of sweet, I guess. I just wish he'd leave me alone. God didn't tell me to marry Hosea. Don't I get a choice? Yes, I do. That's why I kept running away. But it's nice to be loved. Real love. None of those other men care about me like Hosea. And he's obviously determined that we'll be together. Who knows, maybe this time I'll stick around for a while.

LIFE APPLICATION:

- Real, unconditional love means there's nothing you can't be forgiven for. Nothing. Yep, even that.
- Love is a choice.
- Love is a verb.
- If you love yourself, you won't be in an unhealthy relationship.
- The things we value and love, we take care of.

(The Other) Tamar

(Genesis 38:1-30)

BUT FIRST, SOME BACKGROUND:

Tamar (not the one who was raped by her half-brother, the other one) was seriously unlucky in love. Her first husband, Er, was killed by God for being wicked. It was a cultural thing that the widow would be married by the next available relative, so Er's brother, Onan, married Tamar.

Tamar's father-in-law, Judah, told Onan that he really needed to consummate his marriage to Tamar, and fast. If she was pregnant and Er was believed to be the father, that kid would get a serious chunk of inheritance. But if there was a possibility the kid could be Onan's, then Onan would get the whole shebang.

It seems these boys of Judah's are just incapable of pleasing God, though. Onan thought he'd pull a fast one by... well, pulling a fast one. Coitus interruptus. God was not impressed and killed him too.

That left one son—Shelah—to carry on the family name. And it was prophesied that Judah's bloodline would be hella important in the future, so that's pretty crucial. Too crucial for Judah to give over his last living son to the apparently cursed Tamar, so he told her to go back to live with her parents as a widow and wait until Shelah was older. He continued putting her off that way for years.

I am absolutely *fuming*. My father-in-law is a liar. He told me that if I came home and waited, I would be able to marry Shelah when he was old enough. Liar! Shelah is old enough, and I'm still sitting here in my mourning dresses. I should be a bride again! Does he not understand how important it is that his bloodline carries on? I'm doing everything I can to make that happen, and I get thwarted at every turn. But I refuse to give up.

My mother-in-law is dead, and Judah is a widow now. A friend told me that he's setting out for Timnah to sheer his sheep, and that presents me with the perfect opportunity to set my new plan in motion. I change into a nice dress—modest black widows bullshit isn't going to work for this. I cover my face with a veil and wait for Judah on the road to Timnah.

Yes, okay, I'm dressed like a prostitute. But that's the point! Judah is a widow, so my plan is to tempt him into propositioning me. And hot damn, it works.

"What will it take for you to lay with me?" he asks with basically no lead up. This was almost too easy.

"Well, hey there handsome. What are you offering?"

"I'll give you a kid goat from my flock. I don't have it with me, but I'm good for it."

I pretend to think it over for a few seconds before asking what he'll leave with me as collateral. I am a businesswoman, after all.

We settle on his leaving his signet ring, staff, and cord.

Three months later

Well, this backfired. I mean, I'm pregnant, which was part of the plan, but I'm also in jail, which was definitely *not* part of the plan. When word got out that I'm expecting, I was accused of being a prostitute. How else could an unmarried widow be having a baby this long after her husband's death? The irony of this accusation isn't lost on me, I assure you.

A friend rushes in and whisper-yells, "he's demanded they burn you."

"He's literally the worst father-in-law ever," I reply. That's right, Judah, my baby daddy, is calling for me to be roasted. What an ass. "Okay, I need you to do something for me." I scribble on a slip of paper, then hand it through the bars. "Get the box out from under my bed. In it, you'll find a signet ring, a cord, and a staff. Take those things and this note to Judah." You see where this is going, right?

I'm no prostitute, and you know it. These things belong to the man who got me pregnant.

He can't get rid of me now.

LIFE APPLICATION:

- Even with the best of intentions, deceit is still deceit.
- It's always good to have a plan. It's never good for that plan to include manipulating or tricking people into doing what you want.

Sapphira

(Acts 5)

It's exciting to be a part of this growing community of believers. My husband, Ananias, and I are the new kids on the block, and everyone has accepted us. No cattiness or gossiping or jealousy keeping people apart. I know—shocking, right? We cook for each other, help out with kids and homework, camelpool to work, borrow tools from each other—we've got each other's backs. We're family. It feels good and right.

Our friend, Barnabas, sold some land and gave all of the proceeds to the church leaders. That was pretty cool of him, and a few people are following his example. It's not a requirement, but we all want to help the leaders and the community because they've done so much for us. People can give any amount they want, and there's always enough for everyone.

My husband and I recently sold a piece of property for $600. We said we would give it all to the church, but we also want to buy this camel we've been saving for. He's a beauty. He's won several races, and he comes from a great bloodline. We have almost enough to buy him with our savings, but if we take just a little from the proceeds from selling our land, we could have him tomorrow! I mean, it's our money, really. We can do whatever we want with it. We'll just tell Peter and the gang we sold the piece of property for less than what we really did. They'll never know.

My husband decides he will be the big man and go make a big production out of the money we're giving. He's prone to showing off like that. Meanwhile, I'll be getting the barn ready for our new camel. I'm so excited! I can't wait to show him off to our friends.

Where is that man of mine? It's been three hours. How long can you brag about giving money?

I walk to the area where Peter is usually hanging out. It's eerily quiet along the way. Too quiet. Like someone died or something.

As I approach the door, Peter greets me and welcomes me inside. I look around for my husband, but he isn't there. Maybe he stopped by the store to get some things for our new camel.

Peter asks me how much we sold the property for.

I don't hesitate in replying, "Oh, we got $500 for it!" I hear gasps from the bystanders. They must be impressed with the amount of our gift.

"Why did you lie to God?" Peter asks.

Those were the last words I ever heard.

LIFE APPLICATION:

- Ananias and Sapphira both literally dropped dead after lying—that shit can get you killed.
- How you do one thing is how you do everything.
- Do the right thing in all circumstances.

Sitidos, Wife of Job

(Job 2:9-10)

BUT FIRST, SOME BACKGROUND:

Job was a good and prosperous man. He was a devout follower of God, a righteous man blessed with a large family and material things. He and his wife had seven sons and three daughters, and they lived in a nice, big house and wanted for nothing.

One day Satan pays God a visit, telling God that he's been roaming around the land. God asks, "Did you see Job while you were down there? He's one of a kind—Godfearing, blameless, and upright."

Satan considers this, then suggests that it's easy for Job to be so faithful because he has literally everything he could ever want. "I bet if you took all that stuff away, he'd curse your name like any other Joe-Schmo."

"Fine," God tells him, "see for yourself. You can't kill Job, but otherwise do your worst. You'll see."

My life sucks. Seriously. FML. A couple of months ago everything was perfect. I loved my husband. I had

127

ten beautiful, amazing children. I had a huge house full of gorgeous, expensive things. We were all healthy and happy, and every day our bellies were full of delicious food. Now? Nothing. I have *nothing*. My children are dead. All ten of them. My house is gone. My beautiful things are gone. Our servants are all dead. All of our money, our friends, our reputation, gone.

Today I've been begging in the market. Me, begging. Can you even imagine? But that's what it's come to. Job can't work—he's covered from head to toe in painful sores. He can't do anything but sit in the ashes where our home used to be.

"I got some bread," I tell him when I return. "It's not much, but it's all I could get today."

"God is good," he responds as he reaches for the bread. No "Thank you, Sitidos," or "I'm lucky I have such a caring wife," or even, "Only a little bread? But we're starving!"

I could handle it if he lashed out, if he got angry. I'm angry. And I'm tired. And I really just can't take it anymore. All of that anger and sorrow and desperation explode out of me.

"Dammit Job! Why don't you just curse God and die already? Put us both out of our misery!"

I probably shouldn't have said that. But it doesn't make him angry. A little, maybe—he did call me foolish. But he says, "Should we only accept the good stuff from God, and not the bad?"

And that was the proverbial straw that broke this camel's back. I can't do this anymore. I *won't* do this anymore. I go lay in the field with the cows and wait for it to all be over.

LIFE APPLICATION:

- Life seriously sucks sometimes. A lot. Laying down with the cows and waiting for death is never the answer.
- At one point Job does wish he'd never been born, but a friend points out that, while shit's pretty sideways at the moment, he shouldn't discount all of the good he's done prior to this point. Sometimes you just need a good friend to help you find the rainbow when you're in the midst of a storm.
- You've survived 100% of your worst days. And you'll survive the next one, too.
- The bad stuff always ends. If Sitidos had found a way to hold on a little longer, she would have seen that. Job's suffering ended and God rewarded his faithfulness by putting his life back together in a way that was even better than before. He remarried, his children were restored to him, and he lived a long, good life.

Jezebel

(1 Kings 21; 2 Kings 9:30-37)

I'm your worst nightmare.

I'm not a housewife. I'm the RULER of this house... and this kingdom. My husband, Ahab, is king, but let's be honest: He couldn't do this without me. I'm the neck that turns his head. He's weak. He's a pussycat compared to me. He needs a strong woman to command him and to control this crazy-ass kingdom.

I'm a Lebanese princess and lived a life of luxury before I married Ahab. My culture is very progressive, and we worship many gods. Ahab was a prince at the time we married. A prince of Israel—a very conservative and backward society. Our marriage was arranged to create a political alliance between the nations of Lebanon and Israel. And no one saw any potential issues with this?

Israel worships one God—Yahweh. I don't. I continue to worship my nature god, Baal. Ahab didn't care, but that didn't set well with the ~~peasants~~ citizens. They're the biggest whiners and complainers I've ever met. They need to loosen up and live a little. They have so many rules. One God, lots of rules. Many gods, no rules. I prefer to make my own rules, thank you very much. My current ninety-day goal is to rid the kingdom of Yahweh's prophets. Popularity polls show me hovering near zero. Think I care? Hell-to-the-no. I definitely do not. In fact, I'm on a mission. I've brought in 850 of my own Baal prophets and ordered the murder of Yahweh prophets—especially one prophet in particular named Elijah. He is a pain in my royal ass, so he really needs to die. Meanwhile, the hubs is oblivious and has decided he wants the vineyard close to our house. I like wine, and Baal knows I'll need a drink after all of this is over. Ahab offers Naboth some money for his vineyard. Naboth refuses because it's his family's land. He doesn't want to give it up. Ahab just sulks away. When he tells me what happened, I'm appalled. Not at Naboth, at Ahab. You're the frickin' *king*. You can have whatever you want!

Obviously, it's up to a woman to get this job done. I make up charges against Naboth, sign Ahab's name to them, and have him condemned to death by stoning. I take his land and give it to the King. There, done, easy.

Elijah comes to town. *Oy vey*. What now? He says Ahab is a bad man, and he and all of his heirs will be killed. And dogs will eat me. Say what? That's f—ed up. Elijah *really* needs to die.

Long story short, there's a showdown between Elijah and my prophets. Elijah wins. He made a mockery of my prophets, and then he massacred them. Not cool, Elijah. Not. Cool. You just signed your death warrant. You'll be dead by this time tomorrow.

Elijah hears what I have planned for him and runs for his life. He's smarter than I thought.

Ahab has finally gotten a backbone and is living large, throwing parties and worshipping idols. I love it when he takes charge and gets wild like this.

But it doesn't last. Should have known it was too good to be true.

Ahab is killed in battle *just like Elijah said.*

Some punk name Jehu is promised the throne if he can take me out. Hit me with your best shot, baby.

I hear Jehu is in town. I dress up in my finest attire and get my hair and make-up done. Am I seducing him in order to stay alive? Or do I know my time is up, and I want to go out my way? Stay tuned.

Jehu arrives and sends my eunuchs up to me. Apparently, Jehu's not taken with my charms. My own eunuchs throw me out my window, the traitors, and I land on the ground below writhing in pain and anger. I hear horses coming at me, but I can't move fast enough. I try to duck and cover my head...

Narrator in Lady Whistledown's voice:

Dear Reader,

And so Elijah's prophecy came to pass. Jehu victoriously entered the palace and celebrated with food and drink. When he eventually got around to having Jezebel's body taken for burial, the servants were only able to retrieve her skull, her feet, and the palms of her hands. Her flesh had been eaten by stray dogs – *just like Elijah said.*

LIFE APPLICATION:

- To ignore wise counsel and/or warnings is to put yourself at risk of losing everything—including your life.
- Your way isn't always the right way.
- You don't always need to have your way or to be right.

Rebekah

(Genesis 25:21-27:45)

These twins are going to be the death of me.

I know that sounds ungrateful. I was childless, and my husband, Isaac, prayed. Well, he did more than pray if you know what I mean. And then, BOOM, twins. But these guys really seem to be going at it in my belly. It's like a Saturday Night Rumble. It's so bad that I'm to the point I'd rather die than have Hulk Hogan and The Rock going at it inside me all day, every day. I can't take it anymore!

I ask God what the heck is going on with these two. I should have just stayed home—He didn't have good news. He said these two will never get along, and the older one will serve the younger. That's not how it works in our culture. The older one gets the blessing, and younger one serves him. Well, that's just great. I thought I wanted kids, but this is more than I want to deal with. It's too late to abort. I can't seem to die. Maybe they'll come early. Maybe I won't survive childbirth... Maybe I'm being a little overdramatic, but then again, maybe not.

I go into labor. It's god-awful. No pain block. If the midwife tells me to breathe one more time, I'm gonna kick her in the face.

The first one arrives. He's red and hairy. We name him Esau which means "hairy." We're original like that.

The weird thing is that the second one arrives clutching the heel of his brother. That was a little painful for me. We name this one Jacob, which means "heel," because... you get it by now.

They fight constantly. They're opposites in every way. Esau is hairy; Jacob smooth. Esau is an expert hunter and loves the outdoors; Jacob... not so much. He prefers to hang out at home with me, cooking and reading. I know, parents aren't supposed to have favorites, but we do. Esau is Isaac's favorite. You already know who my favorite is. Some say Jacob is a momma's boy. He is. His momma loves him so much. I'd do anything for him.

Jacob is cooking stew one day. He's become a pretty good cook. Esau comes in from the fields or wherever he's been—I don't really care, to be honest—and he asks Jacob for some stew. Jacob says no. And the fight begins. Will these boys ever get along? Don't answer that.

"Jacob, I'm famished! I'm going to die of starvation if you don't give me some stew."

"Tell you what, Esau. I'll trade you a bowl of stew for your birthright." That's my boy—always thinking. He sees an opportunity and pounces.

Esau, on the other hand, isn't a thinker. He's impulsive and lives in the now. "What good is my birthright if I'm dead? Fine, whatever, you can have it. Just give me some stew!"

Jacob hands him a bowl of stew. Esau eats and leaves. Life goes on. A typical day in the Isaac Family household.

Isaac is getting old and blind and thinks he's near death. He wants to give his blessing to our oldest son, Esau. Isaac tells Esau to go kill his favorite game and bring it back and cook it for him, and then he'll give him the blessing. *Oh, no, you're not!*

I tell Jacob to go kill a goat and bring it to me. And *hurry!*

Jacob brings back the goat, I cook it, and then I take the goatskin and put it on Jacob's smooth hands and neck. I put Esau's clothes on Jacob and send him to Isaac with the goat stew. I think he'll pass for Esau—Isaac is blind, after all.

When Jacob approaches Isaac and tells him he's Esau, Isaac doesn't believe him because it's Jacob's voice. Then Isaac touches Jacob, smells him, and decides it must be Esau after all because of all the hair and outdoorsy smells. He gives Jacob the blessing and says his brother will always serve him. Jacob leaves. Smirking the whole way. Game. Set. Match.

Esau arrives right after Jacob leaves and tells his father to get up so he can eat the food Esau brought.

Isaac is confused. He tells Esau what just happened. Esau flips out. He begs his dad for a blessing, too. He's such a whiney-hiney. Isaac tells him, "Here's your blessing: you'll always live by your sword, have barely enough to eat, and will always serve Jacob." Esau is pissed and out for revenge. He wants to kill my precious Jacob.

I tell Jacob to run for his life and stay at my brother, Laban's house. Once Esau forgets what Jacob did to him, he can come back home. What neither of us know at the time is Jacob is in for the surprise of his life. You'll read about him in these pages—if you haven't already that is.

It's hard to live with Esau after this. I don't know if he knows my part in all of it, but I'm sure he suspects it. Sorry, not sorry.

LIFE APPLICATION:

- You reap what you sow.
- What goes around, comes around. When you lie and deceive, you have to constantly watch your back.
- Karma is a bitch.

Delilah

(Judges 16)

I'm a valley girl. I live in the valley between Israelite and Philistine territory. There's this guy from Israel named Samson, and he's, like, totally in love with me. I don't mind though. He's crazy strong. And hot—so hot. Reminds me of Jason Momoa. All that long, beautiful hair; those big, muscley arms; piercing, light-colored eyes; and those abs... Can someone turn on a fan? It's suddenly gotten swelteringly hot up in here. I may need a cold bath after this.

Like I said, he's in love with me. I'm in love with his body and what it can do for me. He's kinda clingy and needy. Not my style. But he is very easy on the eyes.

He's, like, the strongest man in the world or something. No one can figure out where his strength comes from. He's always busting up the Philistines and their stuff, and the Philistines are constantly trying to capture him or kill him, but they can't. He's too strong. But now they think they've found his weakness: he has a thing for Philistine women. That's where I come in. Not because I'm Philistine or anything. I don't define myself as a race—I'm just me, Delilah. But Samson's been visiting me. A lot. The Philistines have noticed.

When Samson isn't around, they stop by and offer me, like, over three thousand dollars to find out Samson's secret. That should be easy enough. I tell them, "Samson is stopping by later tonight. Why don't y'all just hang out close by. You'll have your man in, like, no time."

We're lying in bed. ~~He's smoking a cigarette.~~ We're all cuddled up, kind of dozing off, and it's the perfect time to ask.

"Jason, I mean, Samson... where did all of your muscles come from? You work out a lot? You have a celebrity trainer? You take steroids or what? What is your secret? Is there anything that could tie you up that you couldn't get out of?" I twirl that gorgeous hair of his around my finger. "Like, you know, maybe some bondage or something? Want to try some of that sometime?"

"That sounds like fun. If you had seven bowstrings that haven't been dried out, that would do it. Tie me up with those and have your way with me," Samson responds as he's falling asleep.

The Philistines are listening in on our conversation, and they waste no time. They run out, get the bowstrings, and bring them to me. I tie up a sleeping Samson while they hide around the corner waiting. Once everyone is in their place, I yell, "Samson, the Philistines are here to get you!"

Samson jumps up, breaks the bowstrings like nothing.

What the..."You played me, Samson. What's up with

that? Why'd you do me like that? Be serious. What could tie you up and keep you tied up?"

He grins cheekily and tugs a strand of my hair. "You're so cute when you're mad, Delilah. Okay, okay, I was just playing. It's really ropes. New ropes. If you tie me up with new ropes, I'd be helpless."

Samson drifts back off to sleep. The Philistines bring me new ropes. How they do this so quickly amazes me. I don't understand why they don't just tie him up themselves. Are they afraid? It's okay with me, though. It gives me another chance to touch that smooth skin, those hard muscles... I eventually get him tied up again.

"Samson, the Philistines are here! Help!"

Samson gets up and breaks the ropes like they were a piece of thread. Seriously?

"Ja... Samson, stop playing games with me. I want to know your secret."

"Alright, alright. It's my hair. If you weave it into that loom over there, I won't be able to do a thing. Since I'm awake, how about a repeat of earlier. You know when you did ...."

Oh, yes, I do know. Happy to oblige, ~~Jason~~. Oops, I did it again.

Once he's asleep again, I weave his hair into the loom with the fabric. "Samson, the Philistines!" Samson jumps up and easily pulls his hair from the loom and fabric.

Okay, now you're pissing me off. Tell. Me. Your. Secret.

I nag him about it every time I see him. Then I decide to play the love card.

"Samson, you say you love me, but you won't tell me your secret. You're just playing me. I thought I actually meant something to you. If you really loved me, you'd tell me your secret."

He takes a deep breath and is clearly struggling with whether or not to say something. I pout and try to look really sad and hurt. He lets out a sigh. "It's a little embarrassing, Delilah. I've never had a haircut in my life. If a razor touches my head, that's it. It's all over. I won't have any strength."

I know he's telling the truth this time. While he's in the bathroom, I send someone to get the Philistines. They wait outside until I signal them. Once Samson is asleep in my lap, I motion for the Philistines to come in and cut off his hair. *His beautiful hair.* Can't think about that. I'm waiting for that money they owe me to hit my palm. Cash me outside.

Once the hair is gone, I tell Samson to wake up because the Philistines are here. He can barely raise up because his strength has gone. The Philistines grab him, gouge his eyes out, and take him away.

Don't hate the player. Hate the game.

LIFE APPLICATION:

- Our selfishness impacts others.
- Our greed can hurt others.
- Samson's hair grew back and his strength returned. Your gifts and callings can never be revoked. You may have setbacks, and some of

those setbacks may be because of choices you've made, but God can and will honor the gifts within you. Don't give up on yourself.

Afterword

One of my favorite scriptures is Judges 16:22, *But his hair began to grow back.* This scripture is referring to Samson—he had that encounter with Delilah you read about earlier.

Samson broke a vow and cut his hair (the "source" of his strength). His eyes were gouged out, and he was imprisoned and forced to perform like a circus animal for the Philistines.

There are consequences to our actions.

But his hair grew back.

His strength returned, and he ultimately brought the house down on the Philistines. Literally.

Yay for Samson! But what about you?

You may have broken a vow.

Walked away from commitments.

Done things you thought you'd never do.

You may have forgotten your purpose or have been living someone else's dream for your life.

Your hair will grow back.

God's plan and purpose for your life is still on track. It may look different now, but that's okay. Things will turn out better than your wildest dreams!

Don't give up on yourself—or on God. It's never too late.

Everything is 100% possible, 100% of the time.

Your hair is growing back.

DISCLAIMER

While we've attempted to keep this book as close to scripture as possible, let's be real: the stories in the Bible were written and collected by a bunch of old dudes who left out a lot of details—as men are sometimes prone to do. We've added interesting facts from the Apocrypha and other historical literature—plus a little of our own flair—to put the stories in context for a modern-day reader.

Our intent was to write this keeping the spirit of the story while making it applicable for today.

In short, we left out some "jots and tittles." Get over it.

Acknowledgments

Writing can be a lonely endeavor, but I was never alone. I'm taking this opportunity to publicly thank the people who've made the journey to here possible:

First, my parents, the Reverend Bill and Sybil Thomas, who have always believed in me. Dad left us three years ago, but his legacy remains. Mom still writes me encouraging texts on a weekly basis. No, neither one would approve of the language in this book, but they will understand the heart behind it. They're the first people to realize their daughter doesn't do things the way she's "supposed" to. Don't blame them. They did their best.

Secondly, my husband, Wesley Richards, who lets me do my thing, believes I can do anything, and is always ready for an adventure. He always brings the fun.

Thirdly, the various Church Ladies who joined me in the strip clubs at various times over the past twenty years. Each one of you has a special gift and calling. Thank you for sharing your time and hearts with the girls in the clubs. Thank you for your faithfulness.

Next, Kim, Tammy, and Stacy (aka my "help me bury" friends) who believe in me and encourage me whenever I have a "wild hair" idea.

Lastly, but really first, is God. Back in 1991, when I was testing Him to see if He really was Who my parents said he was, we made a deal. Well, I told him, "Here's the deal: you do your part, I'll do my part. Oh, and you have 30 days to prove yourself." He proved Himself within 3 days. And He's stuck with me now— that was part of the deal. I don't regret making this deal. He's been Faithful more times than I can count.

When this book idea popped into my head in December 2020, I had very little time to write, edit, and print, because I wanted to hand this out as a gift at the Annual Gentlemen's Club EXPO in May 2021. Coaches Cayla, Madison, Ichel, and Sara helped me with mindset, motivation, planning, and strategy.

Jordan Loftis, from Story Chorus, graciously gave me insider tips on how to get this done in a timely manner.

Ashley Casiday, Editor Extraordinaire and so much more, thank you for making my random thoughts make sense. You caught my vision. You're a gifted writer and total Badass Babe, and I hope we can work on future projects together.

JohnEdgar.Design created the cover and helped me get this to print on time.

Ann-Marie Smalley allowed me to use her photo for the dedication page. She's the epitome of a Badass Babe.

The way it all came together, it had to be a God-thang.

Thank you all.

Drenda

If there is anything in this book that has helped you, I would love to know what it was, and how it changed your story.

If you liked what you read, please drop an honest review wherever you procured this book! Your feedback is invaluable.

You can reach me through our website.

About the Author:

Drenda Thomas Richards is as unconventional as this book. She started Jesus Loves Dancers, a ministry into the strip clubs in Houston in 2000. She hosts a podcast called "Taboo Talks" where she and her guests discuss things the church and society ignore like drag queen pastors and dead babies. Drenda helps people navigate a faith crisis, a faith transition, or a questioning of one's faith or spiritual beliefs. She and her husband, Wesley, have been married for seventeen years and have a four-pound Schnoodle named Chassie who has them well-trained.

Find Drenda on these social media platforms:

Facebook – Drenda Thomas Richards

Instagram – Drenda Thomas Richards

Instagram – SacredSoulwithDrenda

Podcast: Taboo Talks